CRITICAL CHOICES THAT CHANGE LIVES

How Heroes Turn Tragedy Into Triumph

DANIEL R. CASTRO

BEARTOOTH PRESS
AUSTIN, TEXAS

BEARTOOTH PRESS
10509 Pointeview Drive
Austin, Texas 78738

Excerpt from *It's Not About the Bike* by Lance Armstrong, ©2000 by Lance Armstrong. Used by permission of G.P. Putnam's Sons, a division of Penguin Group (USA) Inc.

Excerpts from *Every Second Counts* by Lance Armstrong and Sally Jenkins, © 2003 by Lance Armstrong. Used by permission of Broadway Books, a division of Random House, Inc.

Book design and cover by Janice Booker Benight
Manufactured in the United States of America

Publisher's Cataloging-in-Publication
(Provided by Quality Books, Inc.)

Castro, Daniel, R., 1960–
  Critical choices that change lives: how heroes
  turn tragedy into triumph / by Daniel R. Castro.
  p. cm.
  LCCN 2003097051
  ISBN-13: 978-0-97405-431-5

  1. Choice (Psychology) — Case studies. 2. Change (Psychology) —
  Case studies. I. Title.

BF611.C37 2005   153.8'3
                      QBI33-2027

"I shall be telling this with a sigh
somewhere ages and ages hence:
Two roads diverged in a wood and I —
I took the one less traveled by,
and that has made all the difference."

— ROBERT FROST
"THE ROAD NOT TAKEN"

ACKNOWLEDGEMENTS

I would like to thank the following people for taking the time to read those painful first drafts and for being gracious enough to be brutally honest with their comments so that I could separate the wheat from the chaff. Without their comments and encouragement, this book would never have seen the light of day.

James Baker, Rose Berra Castro, Candi Burrows, Rachel Marie Castro, Karen Block, Cindy Bourland, Lynne Dressi, Evonne Jones, Karen Long, Denise Nowotny, Marilee Parsons, Woody "Jack" Roseberry, David Sigmond, Lynne Stoddard, Tamara Thompson, Mark & Susan Walker

I would also like to thank the following authors who graciously and enthusiastically allowed me quote from their great writings:

Lance Armstrong, Laurie Beth Jones, James Balog, Joel Achenbach & Dr. Gerald Mann

Finally, I would like to thank Celia Rocks, who helped me encapsulate the central message of this book into bullet points and develop a keynote speech for a corporate/executive audience.

Many thanks!

To all those brave souls who,
when faced with great obstacles,
made difficult decisions
that changed the course of history...
and those who are yet to be born.

HONORS AND AWARDS

International Latino Book Award

Parent to Parent "Adding Wisdom" Award

ForeWord Magazine
Book of the Year Award – FINALIST

Fresh Voices Award – FINALIST

Independent Publishers Award – FINALIST

HERE'S WHAT READERS ARE SAYING!

CYRUS E. ANGELLOZ – AUSTIN, TEXAS
"If this book doesn't wake you up and stir your soul, you should rush to the nearest clinic and have your vital signs checked."

RANDY GILBERT, AUTHOR OF *Success Bound: Breaking Free of Mediocrity*
"It is said that your life will be the same in five years, except for the people you meet and the books you read. I believe that this book will be life changing for the people who choose to look at life 'through the eyes of heroes' as Dan Castro explains."

MARY JANE HOLT – NEWMAN, GEORGIA
"I boldly predict that the lives of many who read this book will be changed forever, and very much for the better. It should be in every middle school and high school library. It should be in the office or brief case of every executive in the country. Every parent needs it, every child . . ."

J. MCCLURE – WIMBERLEY, TEXAS
"This book can REALLY change your life. A must read!!! You can get so caught up with living your life how everyone else tells you to live it and you are expected to live up to their expectations—not your own. Suddenly, you have lost track of where your life is going. Inspirational, to say the least. It can really bring anyone into a new life, new goals and totally new outlook. You will want everyone you know to have a copy BUT you won't part with yours."

TRACEY JACKSON – GRAFTON, WISCONSIN
"A friend recommended that I read *Critical Choices That Change Lives*. This was an awesome book! It put things in perspective and makes you reflect on your own choices. What makes this book great is he takes simple rules and puts a story to them. The last chapter was the best—believe in your decisions! I would recommend reading it more than once. It is a quick and easy read. I would also recommend this book to everyone, especially business owners. Thanks, Daniel, for an inspiring book!"

WILLIAM E. COOPER – MUKILTEO, WASHINGTON
"Dan Castro has written one of the best books I ever read. The many events average people were confronted with and the extraordinary accomplishments they achieved, often at great personal sacrifice, are both truly motivational and inspirational. They show us what good people are capable of achieving to help others. Mr. Castro has captured the essence and spirit of these men and women and translated it into a book that you won't be able to put down. In today's world it is not often we hear about real heroes—Mr. Castro gives you so many. This book should be in every library, every bookstore, and every college library. It describes decent, honorable, and meaningful people we would all do well to emulate. This book is a must read. Well done Mr. Castro."

KELLI S. McCOO – PORTLAND, OREGON

"One day I was in a very cool book store called Book People in Austin, Texas. You know . . . one of those lazy, summer afternoons when you find yourself all blissed-out with the very, very rare opportunity of time? Time to think about your place here, your life and the bountiful world we create around us. Well, as soon as I walked into the store, I felt this magnetic pull toward the second floor . . . as I rounded the corner up the stair case, I came across this handsome gentle, sweet man in a suit, with this impressively large poster sized cover of a book. It was clear he was getting ready to speak. Not being privy to the topic of this book or if even this bright soul had written it, I checked out the cover and asked if he was going to be speaking soon and if he had written this book? His warm reply cemented my interest in hearing what this intriguing stranger had to share with an intimate group, in a funky book store in Austin, Texas. When the time approached for him to begin, I took my seat quietly at the front of the room. The beautiful little voice inside me said that I was in for a delicious surprise! As soon as Dan Castro stood up in front of the room and began to speak, I was captivated! His beautifully woven tale of how this book came to be was like watching an artist recreate with love and compassion. The light in his eyes as he held the room for more than an hour was so incredibly vibrant, that it made me lean forward with the concentration level of a surgeon. I was so taken by the heart, drive and message coming from this man that the hour felt like only seconds had passed. It was such a gift to have stumbled across this book that I bought two copies that day right after he was done and I have bought three more since, for family and friends. In today's busy world, I know we all wish we had more time to read. Please let me personally assure you this book is worth your precious spare time. Indulge yourself in reading this wonderfully good book!"

TRACY JONES – AUSTIN, TEXAS

"I've read a number of self-help books, and this one really takes the cake. At a time when I was in need of inspiration, I'm so glad I found Dan Castro's book. It really uplifted me and helped me see my way through to renewed hope and inspiration. The way Dan interweaves his many examples and heart-felt, useful advice make the book easy to read and powerful. I had my highlighter handy, because there are so many great nuggets here that I wanted to remember. This is one of the top self-help books I've read, and I've read some of the big ones. This definitely ranks up there with the best. If you need some inspiration that will guide you to feel your inner strength and potential, purchase and read this book. I don't keep a lot of books around, but I think this one will be on my shelf to use as a reference in times when I need excellent advice and inspiration. A truly great book!"

STACEY KANNENBERG - FREDONIA, WISCONSIN

Critical Choices That Change Lives is a life changing book that is a must read for every entrepreneur, family and educator. I have been able to slay several attorneys and the superintendent of my daughter's school this week because Dan inspired me to find my voice and stand up for what I believe in, in the face of opposition and authority. My voice was the correct voice and Dan's book gave me the power to see that sometimes everyday normal people know best. I am no different than Rosa Parks or Martin Luther King, as I too have a dream and my vision is to take back America from corporate greed, a failing educational and legal system, political division and corruption that have left the average citizen uninterested. Enough is enough and I am on a mission of my own to inspire others to read Dan's incredible book and say it's time for everyday people to step up to the plate and be fearless and demand a change. I believe and Dan's book agrees it only takes one person such as a Thomas Edison, Ben Franklin, Walt Disney or an Oprah to believe enough to change the world for the better . . . so why not me!"

DAVID SEFTON – AUSTIN, TEXAS
"A client came to me with horrible problems - family stress, financial problems and an uncertain future. I picked up a copy of Mr. Castro's book for them, as it had helped my family tremendously when we were faced with a period of challenge recently. While waiting for my clients to get to my office, I started reading a few pages. I had forgotten how powerful so many of the stories were."

"Once again, I was struck by what a strong message of hope the book conveyed. Having been a CPA for over 20 years, I am well aware how the stress of financial problems in today's society results in many people considering taking their life. This book is about bleak futures that are turned around through courageous actions. More than any other single book I have ever read, Mr. Castro's book is one of hope."

"The book was so very relevant to many of the issues my clients were facing in their very real today stressful situation—just as it hit home with several members of my family."

"I can recommend this book unequivocally to anyone facing stressful decisions and problems. More than any book I have ever read, it is a life saver."

ROD HARRINGTON – MOOSE JAW, SASKATCHEWAN, CANADA
"Here is a book that isn't only interesting and easy to read...it's downright, powerfully, motivating!"

"When I got to page 47, I had to get up, go to my desk and pull out my yellow marker. Dan Castro wrote something that grabbed me by the horns and shook my thinking. He said:

> *The military has developed 'smart bombs' that have internal maps of where they are going and how to get there. But they only succeed by surveying the territory over which they are traveling and constantly giving themselves feedback to correct their movements. Have we progressed to the point that the weapons we have made to destroy each other are smarter than we are?*

'Internal maps of where they are going.' Is there really something inside me, wanting to laser-focus my destination? 'Feedback to correct their movements.' Am I charging through life blind to the corrections I have to make? Am I wise enough to put some powerful factors into play, those smart bombs of human success?"

"Critical choices. They come to all of us. Crossroads in our lives where we have to decide which way to go. Will I take a chance and run for second base...or will I play it safe, park on first, and merely exist?"

"Castro makes it crystal clear: to make it, to have a life of meaning and power, it's not just important how we think. What makes the difference and changes lives are the choices we make and the actions we take."

"At the end of Chapter 10, Castro says, 'Once you have decided what your goals are, the decision behind the decision is that every day you will repeat a pattern of behavior that you know is slowly pulling you closer and closer to your goals. This is how ordinary people become heroes.'"

"The book's a gold mine. It's not a listing of cute platitudes; it's a book of powerful principles, illustrated by the stories of real people. It's down-to-earth, practical, critical. It's a book to read if you're out to change your life."

Lynne Colwell – www.bloomngrow.net (August 23, 2006)
"Like many inspiring, self-help books, Castro's contains myriad stories of 'success' under fire. But to me, the most important point he makes is that we all face decision points in our lives. We can CHOOSE how we respond. A common thread ties together almost all of those briefly profiled in this book— they chose to act in a 'heroic' manner."

"I was especially interested in Castro's first chapter where he laid out his thinking about the difference between what he defines as 'heroes,' and the rest of us. The secret, he asserts, lies with how they answer three questions: 1) What are you focusing on? 2) What do you believe? 3) What are you expecting?"

"As a life coach, I think these are excellent questions for anyone who wants to achieve anything outside of their comfort zone. In fact the entire first chapter of the book where Castro develops his thesis about why 'heroes' make the choices they do, was informative and helpful. His SEVEN LAWS OF CRITICAL FOCUS™ could be a roadmap for people who are looking for ways to help them meet challenges in their own lives."

CONTENTS

WHISPERS
FROM HEROES

What if you could go back in history and talk to anyone you wanted to about a struggle you were facing? Who would you talk to and why? Jesus? Martin Luther King, Jr? Abraham Lincoln? George Washington? General Patton? Dwight D. Eisenhower? Alexander the Great? Moses? Confucius? Muhammad? Buddha? Mother Theresa? Gandhi? Your deceased grandmother or older brother?

What if those people could speak to you about your current situation? What would they say? Would you listen if they spoke? What if they only *whispered softly?* The voices of our heroes are like whispers in the night. You have to sit still and quietly in order to hear them. They do not preach. They do not lecture. They do not pontificate. They merely tell their stories.

I was once traveling in Belgium on business. I had never been there before. I was wearing a backpack and hauling around a huge black briefcase full of legal files and a five-foot-long suitcase on wheels that felt like it weighed a ton. After I had met with clients over a period of days, I was lucky enough to be in Liege, Belgium, for the first day of the 2004 Tour de France. I had stood or sat in the same place for almost eight hours — right next to the guard rail as the cyclists whizzed by, including one of my heroes, Lance Armstrong.

But now it was almost midnight and I was getting off the train in Brussels after a very long day. I was weak with exhaustion and from not eating much that day. I had no idea where I was going, but I knew the way out of the train station was straight up a long, narrow flight of stairs. I looked around. There was not an elevator or escalator anwhere in sight. I sighed and started my trek up to what felt like the top of Mount Everest. Bang! Bang! Bang! The wheels on my luggage pounded each concrete step one at a time and the sound echoed throughout the train station.

Then I heard a voice with a strong accent. "Here, let me help you." Before I could reply, a hand reached down and grabbed the handle of my briefcase.

"Merci!" was all I could think of to say to the young man who had come to my aid.

"No problem."

"Oh thank God, you speak English! Thank you very much," I said. We were slowly making our way up the stairs, the luggage banging loudly, when suddenly the weight of my one-ton bag disappeared. I quickly turned around to see that another guy had grabbed the rear handle of my five-foot bag and was now helping me carry it up the stairs. *Am I surrounded by angels?* It felt like a thousand pounds had been lifted off my back. "Merci! Merci!" I said.

"Glad to help. You looked like you were having a hard time." *This guy spoke English too!* "By the way, nice jersey," he said.

I looked down and realized I was still wearing the red, white, and blue racing jersey I had bought at the Tour de France in Liege. It had a huge U.S. flag sewn on the front and the letters USA on the back. I felt proud to be part of the team.

When we got to the top of the stairs, the guy behind me said, "Have a safe trip," and disappeared into the crowd. The guy carrying my briefcase said, "Where are you going?"

"I have no idea. But I'm staying at the Novotel," I said.

"Well, then let me help you. I'm going that way and I've been there before."

"No, no. That's okay. Just tell me how to get there." In the U.S., this would have been enough to let the guy off the hook.

"But, I'm really going that way and I know how you feel with all these bags. I'm used to traveling alone with two small children." What a saint.

"Well, okay. I'll follow you then," I said, trying to place the accent. "Are you from England?"

"No, Ireland," he said. He had traveled to Liege to see the first day of the Tour de France just like the thousands of people from all over Europe and the U.S.

We chatted about Lance as we made our way down the dark cobblestone streets of Brussels. He carried my briefcase the whole way and walked me right up to the door of my hotel.

"I don't know how to thank you," I said, still not believing my good fortune. "Are you sure you don't have wings?" I asked, patting him on the back and searching up and down his spine. He just laughed.

I watched as he disappeared down the street, and his words echoed in my ears. "I'm going that way and I've been there before. Let me help you." It left a warm feeling in my soul. That's what heroes do for us.

Every now and then, someone comes along and lifts our burdens and shows us the way. That's what I hope this book does for you.

This book is a collection of stories from the ancient past to the present about ordinary people whose critical choices turn them into heroes. They have been where you are going. They know the way. Let them help you. They have been whispering for a long time. If you listen, they are whispering still.

Some of the people are famous historical figures, some are little-known heroes you may have never heard of. Some of the stories are heart-warming, some are sad. Some are inspiring and some are gripping.

> *"A page of history is worth a volume of logic."*
> — OLIVER WENDELL HOLMES

As I studied and re-studied this collection of stories, I realized that a pattern was developing. Certain principles began to pop out, things that consistently led to victory. I did not make up these principles. I merely stumbled upon them. They have always existed. I have just collected them into one book and organized them in a logical fashion.

I realized that those who survived and prospered in the midst of adversity were able to make the critical choices that others *would not* — because they could see and hear options that others *did not*. Because of this ability, they took courageous actions that made them heroes in the eyes of their families, friends, neighborhoods, and communities.

But what gives heroes the special ability to see and hear options that others don't? The secret is how heroes answer these three critical questions:

1. What are you focusing on?
2. What do you believe?
3. What are you expecting?

These are the three questions behind almost every important decision you will ever make. In this book, you will discover how the answers to these three critical questions determine the outcome of almost every difficult situation you are likely to face. When you read these stories, you will learn how heroes answer these three questions in the heat of the battle — and the tremendous impact it has on the final outcome. The heroic actions you will read about in this book are not necessarily the kind that movies are made about. They are the kind of actions that changes lives — the lives of the actors or the lives of those around them.

In reading these stories, I hope you will begin to see the same patterns I saw. These patterns demonstrate what I call the Seven Laws of Critical Focus™. The Seven Laws of Critical Focus™ explain why some people are able to survive and prosper in the midst of adversity while others do not. Here are the Seven Laws of Critical Focus™:

1. Our most recent *experiences* influence what we focus on, whether we like it or not.

2. What we *focus* on determines what we believe.

3. What we *believe* determines what we expect.

4. We tend to see what we're *expecting* to see.

5. We tend to *filter out* what we're not *expecting* to see.

6. The more we see, the more *options* are available to us.

7. We have the *power to choose* what to focus on,
   no matter what is going on in the world around us.

These Seven Laws of Critical Focus™ are the natural laws that govern what you *focus* on, what you *believe* and what you *expect*—in any given situation. It is my hope that once you understand how the Seven Laws of Critical Focus™ work, your eyes will be opened and you will see and hear opportunities you never have before, you will see new solutions to old problems, you will see alternative paths where others see only dead ends, you will see the blind spots in your life that are holding you back, you will see the bigger purpose behind what you are doing. In short, I hope that you will be able to see *through the eyes of heroes.*

The stories in this book demonstrate that, in each of our lives, there is usually a *decision behind the decision* we are about to make. Sometimes there are several decisions behind the decision we are about to make. Some of these "behind-the-scenes" decisions we make subconsciously without even knowing it. This is an invitation to look deeper, to peel back the layers of the onion and get at the core of the issue.

Throughout the ages, heroic decisions made by mere mortals have changed the course of history. Some of these decisions are well known — the decision of Caesar to cross the Rubicon River with his army, the decision of a collection of colonies to declare their independence from England, the decision of the southern states to secede from the Union, Abraham Lincoln's decision to free the slaves, the United

States' decision to use a nuclear bomb to bring World War II to an end. You may be able to think of others.

However, lesser-known decisions have changed the course of an individual life or changed the course of history for a particular school, town, neighborhood, church, synagogue, or family. Some of these decisions required bravery of the kind deserving of a Medal of Honor. Some have never been recognized except by those immediately affected by the decision.

You may be facing such a decision today. Your decision could change your life forever. It might change the course of someone else's life forever, perhaps someone you love. It could mean the difference between life and death for someone. It could mean the difference between wealth and poverty for yourself or someone else. It could mean the difference between fame and anonymity.

The power to choose is the power to change. The power and freedom to make decisions is one of the most precious gifts we have. Throughout the ages, people have fought wars and sacrificed their lives and fortunes in the name of freedom — freedom to choose how to live, where to go, what to do, where to live, how to worship, what to say, and when and where to say it. You may be facing your own battle for freedom in your own world right now.

All of these people in history have discovered one thing: circumstances alone do not control your fate; *choices do.* Whether the outcome of a crisis situation is positive or negative depends not so much on the circumstances, but in large part on how you deal with the circumstances. Most psychiatrists, psychologists, and behavioral scientists agree with this principle. But this is only half of the *whole* principle. What they leave out is that how you deal with the situation depends on what you can *see* and *hear* in the heat of the battle. What you see and hear in the midst of the battle, in turn, depends on what you are focusing on, what you believe, and what you are expecting. That's why these are the three most critical decisions you can make.

You are an ever-present influence on every situation you encounter. Someone once said, "Wherever you go, there you are." This is humorous but also very true. No matter what situation you may be facing, you bring a force to the table that no one else can bring. That force is you. As you will see in these stories, the outcome of your situation doesn't depend as much on the circumstances as on the *decisions behind the decisions* you make.

My desire is that by reading these stories, you'll find gems of wisdom buried within them. Your job is to learn what you can from *how* the people in these stories saw and heard the world around them.

It may be that no one can really understand exactly what you are going through right now. It may be that no one can truly understand the severity of the consequences of the choices you're about to make. But perhaps you'll gain some comfort and encouragement from the stories in this book. My hope is that you'll learn something from the characters in these stories that will help you in overcoming the obstacles you face. If you listen, they will speak — or at least whisper. If you learn something valuable from this book, please pass it on to a friend.

> **There are no impossible situations in life, only difficult decisions waiting to be made.**

THE DECISION BEHIND THE DECISION

*"The greatest discovery of my generation
is that a human can alter his life
by altering his attitudes of mind."*

— WILLIAM JAMES

Walt Disney and his brothers were physically abused by their father as children. Each of Walt's three older brothers ran away from home one at a time to escape the abuse. During his hours of loneliness, Walt passed the time by drawing imaginary characters. But he did not run away.

When he was eighteen years old, the *Kansas City Star* rejected his application to become a cartoonist. So he took a job as an illustrator with the Kansas City Film Ad Company, which made 60 second animated cartoon advertisements that were shown at movie theaters before the feature film.

In 1923, Walt left Kansas City and went to California and started his own business out of his uncle's garage. He created an animated cartoon character called "Oswald the Lucky Rabbit," and signed a contract with Universal Studios to produce and distribute short films about the furry critter. These short animated films enjoyed great success. But in his youth and naiveté, Walt did not realize that he had signed away the rights to the character. When Walt's contract came up for renewal, Universal Studios refused to renew the contract and announced that it owned the exclusive rights to produce animated films using "Oswald the Lucky Rabbit." Walt was devastated. But on that day, he swore, "Never again will I work for anybody else."

Starting over from scratch, Walt desperately needed to come up with a new character. He drew inspiration from his rodent-infested office. "I do have a special feeling for mice," he said. "Mice gathered in my wastebasket when I worked late at night. I lifted them out and kept them in little cages on my desk. One of them was my particular friend."

Walt created a cute little mouse character that he named Mickey Mouse. On November 18, 1928, the first animated cartoon that synchronized sound with action made its world premier in New York as the opener for a new movie. The short film was called *Steamboat Willie* and it was Walt Disney himself who provided the high-pitched falsetto sound of the little mouse's voice. Mickey Mouse became an overnight success. By 1930, Mickey was a worldwide phenomenon. In Spain, he was called *Miguel Ratoncito*. In Italy, they called him *Topolino*. In Sweden, they called him *Musse Pigg*. Soon, thereafter, Walt started the Mickey Mouse Club that captivated children throughout the world and gave him a captive audience for life. And the rest, as they say, is history.

How did Walt Disney turn his tragic childhood, his rodent-infested office, and his first defeat in business into triumph? He realized what heroes have recognized for thousands of years — few things in life are truly beyond our control. No matter what comes our way, we can always influence the outcome even if ever so slightly. Even during those times in our lives when circumstances and events seem to turn our whole world upside down, the final impact they have on our lives is still largely up to us. The decisions we make determine the final impact. But it is the decision *behind the decision* that is the most critical. Let me explain.

Many behavioral scientists, psychiatrists, and psychologists have analyzed how Viktor Frankl was able to survive in a Nazi Death camp. While Frankl was in the concentration camp, a Nazi soldier noticed that he was wearing a wedding band. He forced Frankl to stand naked in the cold and stretch out his arms. Then the soldier pulled the ring off of Frankl's weak, frail finger, threw it in the mud, and stomped on it. It was the last remnant of Frankl's life as he knew it.

But as he stood there naked, Frankl realized there were some things the Nazis could not take from him: the power to choose his outlook on life; the power to determine *how* he would react to his captors; the power to keep believing and to keep going. The undying belief that he would one day be free was the source of energy that kept him alive until the Allied Forces defeated Germany and he *was* ultimately freed. His choice to believe is what drove his decision not to give up. But there was no reason for Frankl to believe except his *choice* to believe. This was more important to his survival than food or shelter. This was the decision behind his decision not to give up.

There are many more examples of why the decision behind the decision is the most critical one you can make. In the U.S. Army, the Rangers, an elite fighting force, are required as part of their training to go through rigorous survival training in which they must eat bugs and leaves and suffer extreme physical conditions. This training teaches them that they *can* do anything they need to do in order to live. This training builds confidence, layer by layer, and leaves well-worn paths and patterns in their brains that they can follow instinctively if they ever encounter a similar situation in real life. They come to *believe* that even when they are in grave danger, there might be alternatives to death, if they choose to exercise them. When crisis hits, this *belief* energizes their senses and allows them to see potential sources of food, shelter, and weapons that others might not see.

On June 2, 1995, Captain Scott O'Grady's F-16 was shot down by a Bosnian Serb surface-to-air missile while he was trying to enforce the NATO no-fly zone over Bosnia. He was hunted and shot at by the Serbs, but he escaped and survived for six days behind enemy lines by eating grass, leaves, and ants, and collecting rainwater to drink. He was ultimately saved in a harrowing rescue mission. In his book *Return With Honor*, Captain O'Grady relates two stories that were constantly on his mind while he was evading capture and trying to survive.

The first story was about a man who was stranded for eight days in the Arizona desert without food or water. He lost twenty-five percent of his body weight from lack of water. This is normally fatal. His blood was so thick that his lacerations could not bleed. The man had made every mistake in the book. He survived not because of his training or survival skills, but because of his will to live. He simply refused to die.

The second story was about a civilian pilot who was forced to land on a frozen lake in Canada when his engine failed. He was not hurt. He saw a wooded shoreline approximately two hundred yards away, which was a potential source of food and shelter. He started off across the lake and made it halfway, but, not knowing what he would encounter when he got to the woods, he lost hope and returned to the plane. His *belief* that there was no hope caused depression and dismay. Doctors have proven that depression has a severe physical impact on our bodies. It causes our energy levels to drop. It dulls our senses. It prevents us from concentrating and causes short-term memory loss. Depression clouded his five senses and prevented him from thinking about and seeing the obvious sources of food and water. When he arrived at the plane, he smoked a cigar, took a pistol out, and shot himself in the head. Less than twenty-four hours later a rescue team came upon his body. Was it the circumstances that determined his fate or an internal *decision* that there was no hope?

These two stories kept reminding Captain O'Grady that he must keep believing and keep hoping against hope that he would survive and be rescued. It gave him the motivation and the energy to keep struggling no matter what — and it worked. Captain O'Grady survived and became a national hero. The decision behind his decision was to *believe* and keep trying. This belief literally awakened his senses and allowed him to see and hear options that kept him alive until he was rescued.

The U.S. military has learned what the rest of us need to learn: the most dangerous and daunting circumstances alone cannot defeat us. Our circumstances need help from us in order to prevail. It's how we *react* to those circumstances that determines our fate. You can literally turn your fate around by learning to respond properly in any given situation. First you have to make a *conscious* decision to believe that you can survive and prosper. This belief will help you see that there are other viable options besides defeat. Then you've got to make a decision to pursue them.

Nothing affects the world around you like the *actions* you take. Positive mental energy helps, but it isn't always enough. Neither is meditation, prayer, or yoga. You've got to take action, but the actions you take depend on the options that you *believe* are available to you. The available options depend on what you can see and hear in the heat of the moment. What you are able to see and hear depends on what you are *expecting* to see and hear. When you *choose* to believe, an amazing thing happens. It is as though your physical senses are suddenly awakened by a jolt of electricity and you are able to see and hear things you never saw or heard before. How else could Walt Disney look at his rodent-infested office and see Mickey Mouse?

In order to change your world, you must believe that life doesn't happen to you; *you happen to life.* You are not a piece of laundry flapping in the breeze. You have to *choose* to be the cause rather than the effect. You have to *decide* to make something happen.

Life is constantly flowing like a river. If you think about it, you'll realize you never step in the same river twice. Everything is constantly changing. Life is always changing. Sometimes life is good. Sometimes it is difficult. Even if you try to live your life the way you've always lived it, the world around you will change. The river keeps flowing even though you are standing still. You have to go with the flow. You have to adjust.

Once, two experienced kayakers traveled in separate kayaks down the Arkansas River through the world-famous

Royal Gorge in Colorado. The river was at an all-time high because of the heavy snows that winter. The kayakers should not have been on the river that day. As they progressed, they both had to navigate around the same boulders, the same rapids, and the same waterfalls. But suddenly, one of them hit a boulder sideways and hit his head against a rock and died. The other kayaker avoided the boulder and safely made his way down the river. What was the difference between the kayaker who lived and the one who died? Was it the river that determined their fates? Or was it each kayaker's distinct reaction to what the river threw at him that determined his fate?

Like a rapidly rushing river, life seems to keep throwing things at us in rapid succession, giving us little time to think. We suddenly encounter things we weren't expecting, things we sometimes think we can't handle. But, there is nothing in life we can't handle. All we need to do is believe and make a decision. It's all up to us. In life there are really only two choices: win or die. I once saw a sign spray-painted on the side of a rusty, beat-up pickup truck that said: IF YOU AREN'T LIVING ON THE EDGE, YOU'RE TAKING UP SPACE. What a great motto!

Consider the life of Joni Eareckson Tada, who became a quadriplegic as a result of a diving accident. She went from being a young, beautiful, independent, athletic woman to being totally dependent on others for even her simplest needs. When she has a cold, she can't even blow her nose because she can't move her arms. At first she was bitter. She was mad at the world and bitter toward God. However, she has turned this tragedy into a blessing for herself and countless numbers of people. Joni made a *decision*. She formed an organization called Joni and Friends (JAF), whose sole purpose is to help the disabled all over the world. She draws and paints beautiful pictures with the only resources she has left: her mouth, her eyes, her creative mind, and all of her heart. She has written over twenty books and speaks to thousands of people, helping, inspiring, and motivating them to transform their tragedy into triumph. Her life is a testimony to the fact that no matter how horrible the tragedy you may have experienced, you can rise above it.

Joni's story teaches us that whether you're a winner or a loser is a mental attitude. It's an intentional *decision* you alone make. The choice is yours. Joni's response to what happened to her has breathed energy back into the souls of many people who thought their lives were over. Joni made a *decision* that her life wasn't over. It had only just begun.

Look at Candy Lightner, whose daughter was killed by a drunk driver. She could have spent the rest of her life sulking. But, instead of being mad at the world, she made a decision. She decided to form an organization called Mothers Against Drunk Driving (MADD) to turn the tide of the very forces that took her daughter so that other people's sons and daughters could be spared. This is a classic example of turning a negative event into a positive force, and improving your own life and the lives of others as a result. This can only happen when we make an internal decision about how to react to what has happened to us. Neither our circumstances nor our feelings about those circumstances should dictate the final result.

Consider Christopher Reeve, who after his tragic horse-back-riding accident decided to become a spokesman for the disabled and to help raise funds for research into the reversal of spinal paralysis. Look at Magic Johnson, who decided to turn his HIV diagnosis into an opportunity to teach young people and adults about the dangers of AIDS and the importance of safe sex. Look at the legendary cyclist Lance Armstrong, who decided to turn his cancer diagnosis into a fund-raising platform for cancer research.

All of these people could have chosen to wallow in self-pity. They could have chosen to believe their lives were over. But they made a different decision. They decided they could control the impact their personal tragedy would have on their own lives and on the lives of those around them. They decided they had the power to write the final chapter.

Ludwig van Beethoven decided to write his Ninth Symphony even though he was almost entirely deaf. George Frideric Handel decided to write the Hallelujah Chorus while paralyzed from a stroke and hiding from his creditors. What financial challenges are you facing right now? Have you, like Beethoven and Handel, considered what talents and resources you have and what you can do with them? Have you learned to open your eyes and see as they saw?

Something inside each of these people was so powerful and needed to flow out of them so badly that no physical impairment or personal tragedy could stand in the way. These people believed they had gifts that the world needed. But even the choice to believe was a decision. It was the decision behind the decision. Once this happened, it was as though they had grabbed a lightning rod connected directly to God himself. They were able to see and hear opportunities that no one else saw or heard.

By choosing to believe they could make a difference, they tapped into a source of power higher than themselves, and became energized by a source bigger than any external tragedy that could affect their lives. They drank from a well that would fill them up and flow through to others. You see, we often ask life what it has to offer us, when it's really life that asks what we have to offer the world. What difficulties are knocking at your door and asking what you have to offer the world right now?

There's an ancient story from Hebrew history about a widow and her son who were destitute and hungry. All they had left was a flask with very little oil in it and a little flour in a barrel. It was just enough to make one loaf of bread. One day, a prophet visited the woman and asked her to make him some bread. When she told him her bit of oil and flour were all she had left for her and her son to eat, the prophet promised that if she used what little she had left in God's service, she would never run out. In her heart, she believed the prophet. She poured out her last drop of oil and used her last bit of flour to make the prophet some bread. When the prophet had eaten, he told the woman to go back into the kitchen and make some bread for her and her son. Out of faith, she went back into the kitchen to inspect the flask and the barrel. When she turned the flask over, more oil came out, and when she dug in the flour barrel, there was more flour. For the rest of her life, as long as she kept giving, she had plenty for herself and her son.

If you think about it, the same is true for all of us. We have potentially inexhaustible resources within us that we can share with the world. No matter how little we may think we have, when we make a decision to use it to help others, we trigger the force of a higher power that flows through us and ultimately replenishes us.

Think of yourself as a pipeline for water to flow through. If you plug one end, water will fill up the pipe, but it will cease to flow through it. If not used, eventually the water in the pipe will stagnate or dry up and become unusable to anyone. However, if you let it flow, even your own thirst will be satisfied because you're drinking from a well that's constantly flowing. As long as this life force is flowing through us to others, we can't help but enjoy the benefits of it as well.

Each of us has something to give, whether it's time, talent, creativity, or encouragement. You just need to make a decision. Instead of hoarding what you have because you think you have very little, start giving it away. You never know what you have that others might need. As long as you're giving yourself away, your own needs will be met.

A wonderful example of this phenomenon comes from Hattiesburg, Mississippi. In that city lived Oseola McCarty, an 88-year-old African-American woman who had been a washer-woman all her life. She lived in a small home left to her by her uncle, doing laundry for others out of her house for a few dollars at a time. She had a dog named Dog, a hog named Hog, and a cow named Hazel. She had lived by herself since 1967, working every day for a meager income. But she had a great gift — the gift of generosity. Oseola possessed the gift of wanting to help others succeed. On July 26, 1995, she did a very simple thing. She made a decision to give what she had to others, not knowing it would change the rest of her life. Over the years, she'd been saving the little money she made, never wanting much and never needing much. Knowing that she was getting up in age, she decided to dedicate her life savings to the University of Southern Mississippi to finance scholarships. She walked into her bank and asked them to give away her life savings, which amounted to several hundred thousand dollars. She did so without fanfare and without expecting anything in return.

Oseola's generosity made her a national celebrity. Within weeks of her gift, Oseola had been interviewed by every major news organization in the nation. She was on the front page of the New York Times and the Hattiesburg American. She was on Good Morning America and named one of Barbara Walters' 10 Most Interesting People of 1995. She was interviewed by *Tiempo Nuevo,* a live Argentine television show, and featured in magazines such as *Ebony, Jet, People, Guidepost,* and *Glamour.* She was on the BBC and MTV and she carried the Olympic torch a short distance during the 1996 Olympics in Atlanta.

Oseola has received countless humanitarian awards and has met with the President of the United States. Roberta Flack and Patti LaBelle have sung songs for her. Harvard University gave her an honorary degree. Whoopi Goldberg knelt at her feet.

Before her gift, Oseola McCarty had been out of Mississippi only once and she had never been on an airplane. Now she flies all over the country to receive plaques and awards and eat dinner with celebrities. Her friends say that the transition in her life has been like watching the petals of a flower open. People have called her holy. People who talk to her say she makes them feel "clean." They say they feel peace when they're with her. She wrote and published a book of her sayings called *Simple Wisdom for Rich Living.* Oseola McCarty is no miracle worker. She had no extraordinary talent, athletic ability, musical ability, mental genius, status, or social connections to speak of. But she did have the ability to see and hear the world around her as only heroes can. She was not angry at society for her station in life. She did not pity herself. Instead of hoarding what she had to get her through her dying days, she made a decision to give away what she had. She was born into poor circumstances, but she was rich in spirit and has enriched the lives of everyone around her. What do you have to give that you are hoarding for yourself, or worse yet, not using at all?

Better to die knowing that you've made the world a better place than to hoard what you have and die anyway. In this way, your gift lives forever, and your act of love and kindness breathes life into those around you so that they can breathe life into those around them.

Forests are sustained not because the trees keep their energy to themselves, but because they let little bits of themselves, in seed form, fall from their limbs and be carried away by the wind and little animals. By nourishing the lives of everything around them, the trees ensure that they will grow and prosper and that their generations will live on. They replenish themselves by giving themselves away.

This can be true in your life as well. It doesn't matter what cards you've been dealt in life. It doesn't matter what circumstances you were born into, what your parents were like, or even that you may not know who your real parents are. You choose to do with your life what you will. The book of your life is in your hands. The pages in your future are blank until you write something in them. The pen is in your hand. The future is yours to write. In any event, some of the most interesting books are those with plot twists, evolving characters, and surprise endings. It's not too late to change the plot or come up with a surprise ending in your life. You are responsible for how the book ends. At the end of your life, you must stand up in front of the whole class and read what you've chosen to write. In the final analysis, it is as you would have it.

"It is the greatest of all mistakes to do nothing because you can only do a little. Do what you can."
— SYDNEY SMITH

Let's examine the life of Fred Zavala. Fred was raised by his alcoholic grandfather in South Texas in a one-room shack with no furniture in it except a rusty old bedspring. One day a young Bible student, working as an itinerant preacher, came to visit. The student was out to change the world, one person at a time. The student invited Fred and his grandfather to church. Because of the student's warm enthusiasm and zest for life, Fred eventually went to church. It was a small Hispanic Evangelical church.

At church, Fred developed a crush on a girl named Janie. But Janie's father knew about Fred's background and circumstances and was, therefore, not fond of Fred. Fred was never invited to Janie's house when her father invited other church members over for dinner after church. Instead, he would walk slowly in front of Janie's house with his head held low, his hands in his pockets, gazing longingly at Janie's house, wishing he could go in.

Eventually, as the Bible student's time in that little town was coming to end, he tried to get Fred a job so he could learn a trade and earn a living. He succeeded in getting Fred a job at an auto mechanic shop, but things didn't work out there. Then Fred got a job hauling rocks to building sites. Every day, under the hot, burning Texas sun, Fred faithfully hauled his rocks. It was not a glamorous job. But it was a job. He looked on with fascination at the skill with which the stone masons cut and laid the stone to build beautiful structures. He thought, "I'd like to learn to do that." He made an internal decision to learn stone masonry from the masons to whom he carried stone. By watching them and asking questions, he eventually did learn stone masonry. He pursued this craft with passion until his masterful work began to be noticed by others. His work was in such demand that he eventually started his own building business.

Over the years, he did well financially, and he eventually bought houses and land. He even married his dream girl — Janie! He also started a Mexican food restaurant across the street from the nicest steak house in town. Eventually, the steak house went out of business and the bank asked Fred if he was interested in buying the building. Fred did so and he turned the steak house into a thriving business. Now, after church in Mason, Texas, most people eat at either Zavala's Mexican Restaurant or Fred's Steak House. The lonely boy rarely invited to dinner now owns the two busiest restaurants in town.

How did this turnaround come to be? It started with a poor, young college student with a passion for people. He saw what no one else in that little town saw. He saw a jewel where others saw rubble. The vision then spread and grew in the heart of a man who *chose* to believe in a force higher than himself, and who came to believe in his own abilities. It happened because two unique men pursued their dreams with passion, consistent dedication, and blood, sweat, and tears. Neither Fred nor the young Bible student will ever be famous, but both accomplished their dreams. Both have lived happy, fulfilled lives. Fred obtained all he ever hoped for. The student accomplished his goals as well; he helped turn the life of a young man around from that of a poor outcast to that of a wealthy, highly respected businessman in the community. His name is Daniel M. Castro, my father. At my Dad's funeral, Fred Zavala came up to me and said, "Your Dad changed my life."

What is it that you hold in your hand? With the right amount of passion, commitment, and creativity, you can transform your world and the world of those around you. All the resources you need to solve your crises, all the resources you need to achieve your dreams, are within you. But you will not be able to see them until you make a choice to believe.

In a small rural town outside of San Antonio, Texas, there lived a young Hispanic woman named Rosie Gutierrez. Rosie was poor, but she wanted more than anything to put her children through college so that their children would not have to grow up poor like she had. She prayed with all her heart to find a way to earn enough money to put them through college. One day, she got up off her knees and wiped her tears with her apron. Then, she looked outside her window and *saw* what she had never seen before. She noticed that a neighbor had trash piled up in his yard. Yes, the *trash had always been there.* But on this day, the day she *chose* to believe, her eyes were suddenly opened and she saw an opportunity. On that day, Rosie made what would turn out to be a life-changing decision: she offered to carry the trash to the dump for a dollar. She piled all the trash into the trunk of her car and carried it away. This was a dirty, thankless job, but it was sorely needed in that community. Other neighbors began asking for her services as well. She became very busy doing what no one else would do.

Her operation began to grow larger than she had expected. She saved half the money and used the other half to supplement her husband's meager income. She soon saved enough money for a down payment on a used pickup truck and eventually bought an even bigger truck. After a time, she had to hire help.

One day, the city requested bids on a contract for municipal trash pickup. Rosie submitted a bid and to her surprise she won the contract. She beat out all of the national and statewide garbage haulers to get this contract. Eventually she had her own fleet of industrial-size garbage haulers that bore the name GUTIERREZ in bold letters on their sides. In this case, one man's trash literally became another woman's treasure. This woman *made a decision* to use all of her available resources and do whatever it took to achieve her objective. She believed in a higher force, and this faith mobilized all the forces within her and allowed her to see what no one around her saw.

But don't be fooled. The treasure she found wasn't material wealth. The treasure she found was *within* her. The treasure within her gave birth to material wealth the day she *made a decision to believe* and to to get up off her knees and do something about her situation. This was when her eyes were opened. The same is true for us. The treasure we seek is within us, but the only way to find it is through faith, hard work, creativity, and determination. The answers to most of life's problems lie *within* you. You have everything within you that you need to succeed. With this kind of spiritual power and wealth, there really are no obstacles. When you *choose* to believe it, your senses will suddenly be awakened and you will start seeing opportunities you've never seen before.

The point of all these stories is that whatever life throws at you, you have the power to decide what impact it will have on you. But this requires an internal decision. This is the decision *behind the decision* you are facing — the decision to believe. You have the power to write the final chapter. In the final analysis, it is as you would have it. Go forth with courage and tackle the challenges you face. You have everything within that you need to succeed. Now all you need to do is make a decision.

**The decision behind the decision is always
the most critical choice —
and this can make all the difference.**

IT'S *HOW* YOU SEE
NOT *WHAT* YOU SEE

FIRST LAW OF CRITICAL FOCUS™:
*Our most recent experiences influence
what we focus on, whether we like it or not.*

On July 3, 1988, U.S. Navy Captain Will C. Rogers of the USS *Vincennes* issued an order to fire Aegis guided missiles at an unidentified Iranian aircraft headed directly toward his vessel. The unidentified aircraft was destroyed, but it turned out to be a commercial passenger jet. This decision cost the lives of 290 civilians. Many speculate that the Iranians later ordered the bombing of Pan Am flight 103 over Lockerbie, Scotland, in retaliation for the *Vincennes* incident.

What factors were shaping the captain's perceptions when he made that decision? The captain had just been in a surface battle with high-speed Iranian attack boats when radar operators reported that an unidentified Iranian aircraft was descending from an altitude of 7,500 feet toward his ship. His emotions were tense. The First Law of Critical Focus™ was at work. *His most recent experience influenced what he was focusing on.* He couldn't help it. He was focusing on the possibility of another attack.

Before he fired, he sent three warnings on civilian radio frequencies and four warnings on military frequencies. The aircraft failed to respond to any of these warnings. Based on this information, the captain concluded that the intent of the aircraft was most likely hostile. Captain Rogers had to make a decision quickly. He had to choose between the lives of those in the approaching aircraft and those of his own men and his duty to his country. Captain Rogers shot down the aircraft.

> *"Individuals behave not in accordance with reality, but in accordance with their perception of reality."*
> — DENIS WAITLEY

Captain Rogers' perception of the situation was greatly influenced by his most recent experience. His ship had just been attacked. He did everything he could to determine whether the situation was truly as he believed it was. He could not have known the exact identity of the incoming aircraft before it was within range to launch airborne cruise missiles at his ship. He was forced to choose between the lives of his own men and the lives of the people who were aboard what could only be interpreted as a hostile aircraft. He had considered the possibility that the aircraft might be a civilian aircraft, but the jet had failed to respond to all warnings on civilian frequencies. Therefore, he ruled out the likelihood of its being a civilian aircraft. Were the costs of a wrong choice greater than the benefits of a right choice? Hindsight is always 20/20. Had he known the aircraft was a passenger jet, Captain Rogers never would have shot it down. However, if it had been a military jet and he had failed to shoot it down, he would have jeopardized the safety of his men and his vessel.

This story illustrates how our most recent experience influences what we focus on. What we focus on determines what we *believe* as well as our emotional state. What we believe determines what we *expect*. What we expect determines what we *see*. We tend to see what we are *expecting* to see. Captain Rogers saw a civilian aircraft as a hostile military aircraft.

When time was of the essence, the captain quickly did what he could to determine whether the situation was as he perceived it. Even though the consequences were severe, it's hard to fault the captain for making the decision he did.

What kinds of things have the power to affect our focus? Anything that reaches our brains through the five senses:

1. Things that come within our field of vision, whether voluntarily or *involuntarily*.

2. Things that come within our range of hearing, whether voluntarily or *involuntarily*.

3. Things that we touch, *or that touch us*.

4. Things that we taste.

5. Things that we smell.

All of these things combine to create what we call an experience. Our most recent experience affects what we focus on — whether we like it or not.

The First Law of Critical Focus™ is also demonstrated by a story told by journalist Peter Godwin in Zimbabwe. Godwin tells of a critical decision he made while trying to escape the military police of Zimbabwe during his efforts to expose the government's civil rights abuses. He knew the military was looking for him. As he was making his way out of the "prohibited zone," he saw a soldier of the dreaded

Fifth Brigade standing in the road, flagging him down. Godwin quickly ran his options through his mind. He could turn around and head back at full speed. He could dump the truck he was in and run for it into the bush — most of the soldiers weren't terribly fit and it would take them a while to summon air support. Or he could put his foot down on the accelerator and drive straight through. As his options raced through his mind, so did several important questions. Was this a proper stop, with a stronger roadblock fifty yards beyond this lone soldier, or was it a shabby roadblock that he could get away from? How many soldiers were there? What weapons did they have? Did their radio work? (Many troops had faulty radios.) Had this particular group been alerted about his presence in the prohibited zone? Images of being captured and tortured flashed through Godwin's head. That's what he was focusing on.

In the remaining seconds, Godwin decided to go for it. But, as he slammed down his foot on the accelerator, he noticed something that prompted him to double-check his perception against reality. The soldier didn't have a weapon. The Fifth Brigade never moved without weapons, especially in the prohibited zone. Godwin slowed his truck. Then he noticed that the soldier was smiling and that his movements did not seem hostile. Godwin brought the truck to a halt in a cloud of dust. The soldier turned out to be a 2nd lieutenant looking for a ride. Godwin offered the officer a ride and told him he was a local farmer.

A few miles down the road, they came upon a real roadblock, with spikes, a machine gun, and a proper radio antenna shooting into the air. A sergeant of the Fifth Brigade sharply saluted the lieutenant in the truck as they approached and explained that they were looking for a young white man who was helping the dissidents. They were under strict orders to stop any white man, to check his ID, and to question him. It was Code Red. No exceptions were to be made.

The lieutenant got out of the pickup and went to talk to the sergeant. The remaining soldiers had machine guns pointed straight at Godwin, ready to shoot at the blink of an eye, while the lieutenant spoke with the sergeant. After a few minutes, the lieutenant came back and said, "Let's go." Godwin couldn't believe it. The lieutenant told Godwin that the sergeant suspected Godwin of being a journalist spy. But in order to avoid a delay, the lieutenant had convinced the sergeant that the white man he was with was a local farmer whom he had known from a long time back. He had said the two were "old friends." With that, Godwin made it out of the prohibited zone safely, and he later wrote a story that eventually helped put a stop to the civil rights abuses.

Godwin almost made a critical mistake. His most recent *experience* determined what he was focusing on. What he was *focusing* on determined what he *believed*. What he believed determined what he expected. His *expectation* was that soldiers would be looking for him. When he saw a soldier, he saw what he *was expecting to see* — a threat. But, Godwin was smart enough to shake off the blinders of his expectations and truly examine the evidence before him. He *chose* where to put his focus despite what was going on in the world around him. That's when he noticed that the soldier was not carrying a weapon. He saw what most people would have missed.

Godwin compared his original perception to the actual evidence. He quickly sniffed out the clues. He made use of all the available information as well as his quick wit. He didn't panic. He analyzed all the information he had within the amount of time he had. He asked himself all the right questions, and the answers gave him what he needed. He saw things he hadn't seen at first. Then, he made a decision that saved his life several miles down the road. If he had sped past the lone soldier, he would have run into the real roadblock down the road with no ally at his side.

Godwin followed the principles that apply when you are in a critical situation. Here, the decision behind his decision was to stop, even if for only a second, to check reality against what he was expecting to see. That's what made him a hero. Likewise, you have an internal choice to make before you make your final choice. Will you stop and consider the possibility that what you are seeing may have been unduly influenced by your most recent experience and what you were expecting? Will you choose to stop and double-check the evidence? Or will you plunge forward unchecked? Even when there is a true emergency and time is of the essence, you have the option to stop and quickly check your perception against the tangible evidence around you.

Sometimes all of our options seem perilous. There is no clear choice. No matter what we do, something could go wrong. The crux of the matter is that whatever we do, we must be willing to live with the consequences of our actions, whatever they are. Remember, you have to live with yourself for the rest of your life. Can you stand the memory of what you are about to do? Could you recommend it to your children as the best course of action if they were to ask you for advice? Do you want this to be your legacy?

When *you* are in a critical situation, take courage and follow these steps:

- First, realize that you have the option, and maybe even the responsibility, to stop and confirm whether or not things are really as you perceive them to be. What recent experiences are influencing what you are focusing on and your expectations?

- Second, double-check the evidence around you to see if you've missed anything.

- Third, quickly assess all the evidence in the time that you have.

- Fourth, know what questions must be answered before you decide.

- Fifth, if it is impossible to obtain all of the information you need in the amount of time you have, analyze the information that you do have, make educated guesses about the missing information, and follow your training and gut instinct.

When you follow these steps, you will be able to see as heroes see. You may see things you've never seen before and new options will open up that you've never considered. Afterward, people will look back and say you were a hero.

But you will only begin to act as heroes act when you learn to see the way heroes see.

Finally, take comfort in the fact that everything you have experienced so far in life has prepared you for this moment. You may not think so, but you are where you are because you can handle it.

FIRST LAW OF CRITICAL FOCUS™:
Our most recent experiences influence what
we focus on, whether we like it or not.

WHEN HEROES ARE BETWEEN A ROCK AND A HARD PLACE

SECOND LAW OF CRITICAL FOCUS™:
What we focus on determines what we believe.

THIRD LAW OF CRITICAL FOCUS™:
What we believe determines what we expect.

FOURTH LAW OF CRITICAL FOCUS™:
We tend to see what we're expecting to see.

The Bedouin tribes who live in the desert have a story they tell their children that can teach us a great deal about how we make decisions. According to the story, there was once a man living in the desert with his family. He saw a cloud of dust and sand approaching from the horizon and said to himself, "It is a terrible beast coming to eat me and my family!" As the cloud of dust got closer, he saw that it was actually a man dressed in black on horseback. He then said to himself, "It is my enemy, coming to take over my well!" He went to get his rifle to defend himself. The horseman got closer and the man could now see the rider clearly through the sights of his rifle. He recognized the rider and said to himself, "No, it is my brother."

The three lessons of this story are:

1. What we *focus* on determines what we believe.

2. What we *believe* determines what we expect.

3. We tend to see what we're *expecting* to see.

These are the Second, Third, and Fourth Laws of Critical Focus™ at work.

Most people think they are in control of what they believe. But the following stories demonstrate how little control we actually have over what we believe. During the Korean War, the North Korean officers running the POW camps experimented on prisoners by telling those with minor injuries that their injuries were severe and that they were going to die. At the same time, they told those with severe injuries that their injuries were minor and they would surely live. Amazingly, many of those with minor injuries died because they *believed* they could not live. Many of those with major injuries lived because they *believed* they would not die. What they believed determined what they expected. What they expected came to pass because they expected it to come to pass.

How did the North Koreans accomplish this? The POWs had no evidence to contradict what their captors were telling them. Therefore, the only thing they had to focus on was the words of their captors. If someone can control what we focus on, they can control what we believe. What we believe determines what we expect. Sometimes what we believe can determine whether we live or die.

Okay, so you're not exactly a prisoner of war right now. I realize that, but let me give you another example. Have you ever wondered how otherwise rational people sitting on a jury can acquit someone who is obviously guilty? Have you ever wondered how jurors could acquit someone who *actually confessed* to the crime? Let me give you an inside look at how trial lawyers control what jurors believe.

On May 30, 1997, a man named Montoun Hart allegedly tortured and murdered an English teacher named Jonathan Levin in order to get the PIN for his ATM card. After he was indicted, a witness testified that it was Hart who had made a withdrawal from the ATM at the relevant time. Hart also confessed to the crime, describing details that no one could have known unless they were involved. In the face of this overwhelming evidence, the jury found Hart *not guilty and freed him!* The jurors later explained that in the photo of Hart taken after a six-hour police interrogation, it looked like he was "wasted," meaning that he looked drunk, tired, or high. Therefore, they discounted his confession. Make no mistake. There was no evidence of torture or physical abuse by the police during the interrogation. The jurors simply didn't believe the confession. Instead, the defense attorneys convinced them to *focus* on the photograph above all else. What they focused on determined what they believed.

How did this happen? How could the defense attorneys have turned black into white? How could they have persuaded the jurors that Hart was innocent?

Perhaps the best way to explain it is to use a highlight football reel as an example. After a football game, coaches and players review the videotapes of the game to see what went right so they can repeat it and what went wrong so they can avoid it. They also use these films to evaluate a player's performance. Multiple video cameras throughout the stadium capture the players and their actions from all different angles. But you can only watch one film at a time. In addition, the editors can choose which clips to show and which not to show.

Let's say you watched a review film of running back Emmit Smith. In the tape, he fumbled four times. He was tackled behind the line of scrimmage seven times. He dropped five passes, and he had four carries where he only gained five yards or less. What would you believe about Emmit Smith?

Now let's say you watched a different review film of the *same game.* But in this clip you saw Emmit Smith score five touchdowns and rush for over two hundred yards. Now what would you think?

That's the way trial lawyers work. One lawyer shows you the clips of evidence that he wants you to focus on. The opposing lawyer shows you the clips of evidence *he* wants you to focus on. All good trial lawyers know that if they can get you to focus on only their evidence, they can control what you believe. The best trial lawyers are those who can get the jurors to focus primarily on the evidence that they show. A standard motion filed in every jury trial is called a "Motion in Limine." A Motion in Limine is a motion asking the court not to allow the other lawyer to talk about or introduce certain testimony and exhibits that could possibly kill the client's case. But wait! I thought the purpose of a jury trial was to let the jurors see all of the evidence so they can decide who's right. That is the ideal, but it is not the reality. The reality is that lawyers try to keep out all kinds of evidence that you are not aware of. The goal is to get you to focus only on their evidence and completely ignore or not even hear the other side's evidence. If they can control what you focus on, they can control what you believe.

Of course, an actual trial is much more complicated than this, and many factors, such as how believable a witness is, contribute to who wins. But, this is the basic strategy that all trial lawyers use. Why? Because trial lawyers understand the Second Law of Critical Focus™. *What you focus on determines what you believe.*

In July 2002, five-year-old Samantha Runnion was kidnapped from outside her apartment complex in Southern California while she was playing with a friend. The next day, her naked body was found along a nearby highway. She had been raped and then asphyxiated. The man who allegedly committed this crime was Alejandro Avila. This horrendous murder could have been prevented if Avila had been convicted of sexual assault two years earlier.

Two years earlier Avila had been accused of child molestation. Two nine-year-old girls each testified in graphic detail about the abuse they said Avila had inflicted on them. According to the *Los Angeles Times*, one of the little girls said, "When my mom went to work, he would take me into the room and he would do those things to me." She described how he would take off her clothes and his clothes. "Then he would start touching me and then making his private part touch mine," she said.

The defendant's argument was that Avila's ex-girlfriend had encouraged the girls to make up those stories. The defense attorney repeated this theme over and over, day in and day out, throughout the trial. This is a classic strategy used by both trial lawyers and professional marketers and advertisers. It is called repetition — and it's very powerful.

That's why when a company wants to launch a new product, you suddenly start seeing the product everywhere — on TV, in magazines, in newspapers, on billboards — and hearing about it on the radio. The company is controlling your focus *without your consent*. And it works. The evidence shows that the more you see and hear about a product, the more you will tend to *believe* it is a product worth buying. It works the same way in jury trials, and the best trial lawyers are those who are able to control your focus. Do you still think you are *always* in control of what you believe?

Despite the two girls' detailed and graphic testimony, the defense attorney used the power of repetition to convince the jury that the girls just could not be believed — and he succeeded. In jury trials and in life, the Second Law of Critical Focus™ is always at work whether we realize it or not. *What we focus on determines what we believe.*

Did you notice the Second, Third, and Fourth Laws of Critical Focus™ at work in the last chapter in the story of the USS *Vincennes* and the story of Peter Godwin in Zimbabwe? Because the captain of the USS *Vincennes* was *focusing* on the recent Iranian attack on his ship, he *believed* there would be more attacks. Therefore, when he saw an Iranian aircraft, he *expected* it to attack. He saw what he was expecting to see. He saw a peaceful civilian aircraft as a hostile military aircraft. Similarly, because Peter Godwin was *focusing* on the threat to his life, he *believed* that all soldiers were looking for him. Therefore, when he saw a soldier on the road, he *expected* him to be a threat. He too saw what he was expecting to see.

The captain of the USS *Vincennes* made a decision based on his incorrect perception of the situation. This decision cost hundreds of civilian lives. Peter Godwin re-evaluated his initial perception of the situation, and made a decision that ultimately *saved* hundreds of civilian lives. The difference was that Peter Godwin looked for and focused on *new information* that changed his beliefs. Once his beliefs changed, his *expectations* changed. This is how heroes operate. They take control of what they are focusing on.

If we can control what we *focus* on, we can control what we *believe*. If we can control what we believe, we can control what we *expect* in any given situation. What we're expecting in any given situation is critically important because it determines what actions we are likely to take.

In their book, *Inattentional Blindness*, psychologists Arien Mack and Irvin Rock concluded: "When we are intently awaiting something, we often see and hear things that are not there." The brilliant psychologist William James puts it this way:

> "When waiting for the distant clock to strike our, mind is so filled with its image that at every moment we think we hear the longed for or dreaded sound. So it is with an awaited footstep. Every stir in the wood is for the hunter his game; for the fugitive, his pursuers."

If you think about it for a minute, you may be able to remember times when you saw or heard things that weren't there — solely because you were anticipating them. Psychologists have been keenly aware of this phenomenon for many years — *we tend to see what we're expecting to see*. However, it is my position that the Fourth Law of Critical Focus™ applies to *all of life*, not just to things we can see with our physical eyes. As human beings, we tend to see *life*, not as it is, but as we are expecting it to be.

Whenever you find yourself between a rock and a hard place, stop and ask yourself, "What if the situation is not as it appears to be?" How would this change your attitude? How would it change your behavior? How you deal with a situation depends on how you perceive it. How you deal with people depends on what you perceive their motives to be.

In the movie *Crimson Tide*, the characters played by actors Denzel Washington and Gene Hackman find themselves between a rock and a hard place. They are naval officers on a U.S. nuclear submarine deep in the ocean. They've received an order to launch nuclear missiles within a certain amount of time. But due to communication problems they are not able to confirm the order. They have two choices. Either they can launch their nuclear weapons *without the benefit of a confirming order* and risk starting a nuclear holocaust without justification or they can wait to launch their missiles and, in the interim, risk allowing America to be annihilated.

Gene Hackman, as the commanding officer, chooses to launch the missiles. Denzel Washington, as his second in command, argues to *wait for the confirming order*. A critical leadership conflict ensues. The commanding officer is overruled by a technical rule of military procedure and is placed in the brig to prevent his interference. If the subordinate officer is wrong, it will cost him his career and possibly the destruction of America. If he is right, he will have saved the world. Tough choice! In the end, the alarm turns out to be false and the second in command proves to be right. But at the time, neither officer knew with certainty who was right. If the alarm had been real, no rule of procedure could have justified the second in command's failure to save America. They were faced with what looked like a lose/lose situation.

When you are faced with what looks like a lose/lose situation, what factors do you consider? Do you choose the lesser of the two evils? When time is of the essence and people who are counting on you are pressing for an answer, you must ask yourself two questions:

1. What are the consequences if I am right?

2. What are the consequences if I am wrong?

Quickly assess the best and worst case scenarios of each option. Ultimately, when there's no time to think, you must rely on your training, previous experience, and gut instinct. After all, you have to live with yourself when all is said and done. You must be at peace with yourself.

Finally in order to expand the options that are available to you, take control of what you are focusing on. Remember, what you focus on determines what you believe. What you believe determines what you expect. What you expect determines what you see.

SECOND, THIRD AND FOURTH LAWS
OF CRITICAL FOCUS™:
**What we focus on determines what we BELIEVE,
which determines what we EXPECT,
which determines what we SEE.**

WHY WE LOOK WITHOUT SEEING

FIFTH LAW OF CRITICAL FOCUS™:
We tend to filter out what we're not expecting to see.

One morning I was getting ready for work, looking for my casual shoes that I wear with my khaki pants on Fridays. I couldn't find them anywhere. I looked where I always look — in the closet, next to the bed, under the bed, in the living room. I couldn't find them. I looked in all those same places again, thinking I had just overlooked them, but they were nowhere to be found. I thought maybe I was just a little sleepy. I would look again, slowly and carefully. Not there again. I expanded my search. I looked in the kids' room, in my office, in the bathroom, in the kids' bathroom. Nowhere.

Now I was getting desperate. I was going to be late for work if I didn't find them soon, or — horror of horrors! — I would have to wear dress shoes (and a suit to match) on a day when I did not have to be in the courtroom. It was a crisis. But I was strong. I thought I would look in the usual places one more time. And then it hit me. If I kept looking in the same places I had already looked, I would never find the shoes. I was only wasting time, frustrating myself, and making myself late for work. The shoes clearly were not in the places I had been looking. I was in a bit of a dilemma because

I had no idea where to look if the shoes were not where they were *supposed* to be. What were my realistic alternatives?

Something told me that if I wanted to find my shoes, I had to look where I had never looked before, even if it made no sense to look there. When I made the decision to change my pattern to include the out-of-the-ordinary, the first off-the-wall place I could think to look was the garage. I never put my shoes in the garage because I don't take my shoes off before entering the house.

Nevertheless, out of obedience to my inner voice, I opened the garage door and looked around. I was right. My inner voice was wrong. The shoes weren't there. But sitting there as big as day was the car I drove only on weekends. I had driven that car to see my folks the previous weekend. Then I remembered I had taken my casual shoes with me. I opened the car door, and there they were, sitting on the back seat, staring at me as if to say, "I told you so." My inner voice was right after all.

It was then that a light turned on in my head. I stood there staring at my shoes, pondering the lesson that life was trying to teach me. I was overwhelmed with one question. In my life, had I also been looking in the same places over and over for answers that I already knew weren't there? Was I ignoring the messages life was sending me? Was I going in circles in my life, hoping that the next time I passed that way, what I was looking for would suddenly materialize? Was I hoping my same pattern of behavior would somehow produce different results than it always had before? I had actually convinced myself that the things I had been dissatisfied with for years would suddenly improve if I just improved my attitude, gritted my teeth, and kept going.

I suddenly realized that if I wanted to change the results I was getting, I had to change not only the decisions I was making, but also *how* I went about making those decisions. I had to change my actions if I wanted different results. I had to change my pattern of behavior to include things I had never tried before. This, of course, would require considering options I had never considered before — even if in my mind they had previously been inconceivable, illogical, or even *forbidden*. I had to get out of my mental and emotional rut, my regular way of making decisions.

I also learned that my expectations of the way the world *ought* to be don't always reflect the way the world really is. The lesson of the missing shoes is that what we're looking for in life isn't necessarily where it's *supposed* to be. Our preconceived notions don't always work. They aren't always consistent with reality.

Is it possible that what you've been taught all your life isn't necessarily correct? We need to adjust our attitudes to factor in what life is trying to teach us. We shouldn't blindly and ignorantly keep repeating the same patterns of behavior over and over, oblivious to the results. We need to listen to life's wake-up calls. One thing is certain: *When you start looking in places you've never looked before, you will start seeing things you've never seen before.*

The military has developed "smart bombs" that have internal maps of where they are going and how to get there. But they only succeed by surveying the territory over which they are traveling and constantly giving themselves feedback to correct their movements. Have we progressed to the point that the weapons we have made to destroy each other are smarter than we are?

Steve Andreas and Charles Faulkner introduced the idea that "the map is not the territory" in their book, *NLP: The New Technology of Achievement*. The concept is simple but profound. The map is only a piece of paper. The territory is the actual earth, which you are experiencing as you walk through this life. The map is never 100% accurate because the earth is constantly changing. Also, a map is only a perception of what someone else remembers having seen, which you have adopted and have *chosen* to believe. What mental "map" have you been following all your life? Is what you've been taught working for you? Have you stopped to check the "map" against your actual experience? Are you communicating with yourself like a smart bomb to adjust for what you are actually experiencing?

Things happen or don't happen in our lives for a reason. Perhaps something or someone is trying to send us messages. For me, the message was, "You will not find what you are looking for if you keep looking in the same old places. Isn't it about time you looked somewhere else?"

Laurence Gonzales has studied why accidents happen in the wilderness among hikers, kayakers, and moun-taineers. In his profound work, *Deep Survival*, Gonzales explains why otherwise intelligent people miss obvious warning signs that could have prevented the accident and fail to see obvious escape routes and sources of food and shelter. Gonzales explains that, because of how the brain works, if we are searching the house for a red hardback edition of *Moby Dick*, we are not likely to see a blue hard-back copy of *Moby Dick* even though it is staring us in the face. Our mind literally filters out things we are not expecting to see.

Most people assume that they simply see what is there and that they do so by merely opening their eyes and looking. However, psychologists have concluded that in our daily experience we are blind to many objects that may be in plain sight. Psychologists Arien Mack and Irvin Rock call this "looking without seeing" or "inattentional blindness."

My own experience with this happened when I returned home from a trip to New York City. After finding my car in the airport parking lot, I turned on my air conditioner full blast to get some relief from the 105 degree Texas summer. My next challenge was to find the parking meter ticket that would tell the parking attendant how many days to charge me for. It's a tiny piece of paper and I normally toss it in the center console of my car with all the other stuff that sits in the center console. So that's where I looked. I found loose change, paper clips, fingernail clippers, fingernail clippings, dental floss, used dental floss, pens, highlighters, a pocket knife, a comb, receipts, and who knows what else. But no parking meter ticket.

I must have put it in my wallet. Sometimes I write down the number of the parking section I'm in on the meter ticket and stick it in my wallet so I don't have to go through the entire five-acre parking lot looking for my car. My wallet was stuffed full with my business cards, other people's business cards, my driver's license, credit cards, State of Texas Bar card, pictures, long distance calling cards, a Sam's card, cash, and handwritten reminders of things to do. But no parking meter ticket.

I searched the center console again, more slowly this time. Nothing. I decided to take more serious measures and pulled everything out of my wallet and spread it out on the passenger seat. As I was going through this pile, one piece of paper at a time, something blew into my face from the air conditioner, which was still blowing full blast. It felt like a bug was dancing on my nose. I reached up to swat it and discovered that it was a tiny piece of paper. It was the parking meter ticket! *What the hell?* I stared at it in disbelief. Then I busted out laughing.

I remembered I had stuck the parking meter ticket in the very center of the steering wheel where the seams come together so that it would stick out horizontally and point right at me when I sat down in the car. The point was to try to save myself the regular hassle I go through every time I return home from a trip — trying to find the stupid parking meter ticket. But even when it was literally staring me in the face, I couldn't see it. The air conditioner had to make it fly up and hit me on the nose! Why? Because I was not expecting it to be there. I expected it to be somewhere else. My mind had literally filtered it out.

Arien Mack and Irvin Rock explain:

> "Almost everyone at one time or another has had the experience of looking without seeing and of seeing what is not there... During these moments, even though our eyes are open and the objects before us are imaged on our retinas, we seem to perceive very little, if anything."

To confirm this fact, psychologist R.F. Haines conducted an experiment in which researchers asked commercial airline pilots to fly a simulated plane into a landing. As they began to descend for the landing, the computer put another airplane right in the middle of the runway where they were supposed to land. Many pilots tried to land the plane anyway instead of pulling up. Why is that? Haines explains that our mind tends to filter out things that we weren't expecting so that *reality becomes consistent with our expected model of the world.*

When my book editor read this chapter, she concluded that this must also be why it is so difficult to proofread your own letters and reports. You know what the document is *supposed to say* and your mind filters out all of the errors. That's why you need someone else to proofread your work. It is my position that the Fifth Law of Critical Focus™ applies to all of life, not just to typographical errors, looking for a piece of paper, or landing an airplane. As human beings, we tend to see *life* not as it is, but as we are expecting it to be. We look for evidence that supports our expectations and discount or exclude any evidence to the contrary. Then we become frustrated or disillusioned, and we stay frustrated until we reconcile our expectations with the way life really is.

If your mind is capable of filtering out huge obstacles in your flight path, physical objects that are literally staring you in the face, and obvious errors in your reports, *is it possible* that you have been filtering out the things that aren't consistent with your expectations of life? *Is it possible* that you are missing obvious errors in the way you do life? We all have "blind spots" and hidden character flaws that everyone sees except us. They are like the little piece of spinach between your teeth that everyone stares at when you smile. We don't see them because we live inside ourselves. But they are obvious to everyone else.

I have represented hundreds of people who were defrauded over the years. In my research and analysis, I discovered that some of the most intelligent and sophisticated people on the planet have been deceived over the centuries, including doctors, engineers, professors, high-level executives, and even lawyers. I have often asked myself how this could be. In most cases, there were huge red flags warning these people not to invest their money and not to sign the proposed contracts. Yet they plunged headlong into these traps as though there was not a brain cell left in their head. It wasn't until I did the research for this book that I realized the source of the problem.

I realized that if someone waves a big enough carrot in front of us, most people focus on the carrot, which causes us to miss the obvious warning signs or to significantly discount them. When we focus on the benefits rather than the risks, we are more likely to miss the red flags. Once we have made up our mind to focus on the carrot, it doesn't matter that our friends or family may warn us not to take that course of action. We dismiss their concerns by saying they are "just being negative" or they "just don't get it." Then we defend our position by looking for additional evidence that supports what we have already made up our mind to believe, and we discount the evidence that contradicts our position.

Charles Perrow is a professor of sociology at Yale University who studies why catastrophic accidents occur. In his book, *Normal Accidents*, Perrow explains one of the causes:

"[W]e must, of course, make a judgment, even if only a tentative and temporary one. Making a judgment means we create a "mental model" of an expected universe ... You are actually creating a world that is congruent with your interpretation, even though it may be the wrong world.

Although Perrow is attempting to explain one of the reasons why catastrophic accidents occur, the Fifth Law of Critical Focus™ applies to all of life. We tend to filter out what we're not expecting to see. The possibility that our mental model of the way the world "ought to be" may not be consistent with the way the world really is could have staggering and sometimes tragic results.

On the other hand, it is the most incredible feeling of liberation once we realize that we can *consciously* and *deliberately* choose a different and more accurate model of the world. That is the *decision behind the decision.*

It's essential that you come to grips with issues you may have been ignoring for years. You may find that you are going in circles, getting the same results you've always gotten, and waiting for something to change. You're waiting to win the lottery or waiting for that special someone to magically enter your life.

You must be willing to put down the map and study the crushed grass, the broken twigs, and the footprints in the soil of the trail you are on. You must be willing to experiment with things you've never tried before. This may require that you start reading books you've never read before, going places you've never gone before, and meeting people you've never met before.

You've got to take risks. When you alter your pattern of behavior, you never know what you're going to find. But one thing is certain. You will get different results from what you've been getting.

One of the most critical principles I can offer you is this: *Don't hide from the truth.* Accepting the truth is the best and quickest way to deal with any problem. When you ignore the truth, you end up considering options that are fundamentally flawed because they're designed to deal with something other than the true problem. When people deal with something *other than* the true problem, by definition they steer brain power and energy off course. This causes a waste of time, money, and energy. Stop and make sure you are dealing with the right problem.

The true purpose of America's involvement in the Vietnam War was questioned from the beginning. According to Secretary of State Colin Powell, the military should have gone in to win or not at all. Instead, the country spent billions of dollars, and many Americans lost their lives. If our nation's leaders had honestly assessed the situation, there were really only two options: (1) avoid the whole situation, which really had nothing to do with us anyway; or (2) use whatever military means were necessary to win the war as quickly as possible. In recent years, the U.S. military has proven time and time again that they know how to win a war quickly without the use of nuclear weapons. What was stopping them in Vietnam? Tragedy happened because our nation's leaders did not honestly assess the situation or perhaps because they had mixed motives for being at war to begin with.

As another example, I know an older gentleman who has become hard of hearing. Everyone knows it but him. Everyone has encouraged him to get a hearing aid, but it's too embarrassing for him. It would be admitting weakness or old age. Instead, he insists that his hearing is fine and that people simply need to speak more clearly. His hearing problem is hurting him in business because he can't understand his clients, and in his personal life because people get frustrated when he can't understand them. The simplest and most efficient solution would be for the gentleman to get a hearing aid, but this would require that he accept the truth. Ignoring the truth causes frustration and a net waste of time, energy, and resources.

Regardless of the critical situation you're facing, take a long look in the mirror. What do you see? Are you ignoring the wake-up calls? Are you ignoring your inner voice? If what you're doing now isn't taking you in the direction you want your life to go, you have to ask yourself, "Why am I doing this?"

The simplest example of the need to be honest with yourself in making decisions is when you're contemplating buying something. You see something you really want, but you're not sure you can afford it. You haven't balanced your checkbook in a while, but you *think* you have enough money in the bank to cover it. So you buy it and hope you have enough money to last to the end of the month. Then, sure enough, you get one of those thin envelopes in the mail from your bank telling you a check has been returned for insufficient funds, plus the bank is charging you $20 for the bounced check. Or you buy something on credit when you're not sure you can handle the monthly payments and then you get stressed out financially because you can't afford to pay all of your bills. In matters of finance or business, the choices we face can be easily decided for us if we honestly assess our financial situation. This principle applies whether you're an individual managing your checking account or a business owner running a multimillion-dollar business.

The principle here is not the importance of balancing your checkbook, but the importance of honestly assessing the facts before making a major decision. When you honestly assess the facts, you'll be surprised how many issues will be decided for you. It's only when you ignore the truth that you make the struggle of decision-making more difficult than it is.

As another example, if you've been trying to build a small business and your customer base is small and dwindling, it may be time to try something different. This may mean you need to start an aggressive marketing campaign or come up with a new and creative way to serve your customers' needs. Through hard work and determination you may ultimately succeed, but you need to face the facts before you waste much more time and energy pursuing a course that's not working.

Science teaches us that the dinosaurs became extinct not because they were the weaker species, but because they were unable to adapt quickly enough to their rapidly changing environment. Likewise, if we are going to survive, we have to learn to adjust and adapt. There is no preordained course of action that you are *supposed* to take. Learn to adjust to what life throws at you. We all have options. Every course we could take has its own advantages and disadvantages. How good our choices turn out to be is entirely up to us and how we adapt.

Just as important as it is to look outward to the objective factors affecting your decision, you must also look inward and honestly assess what's in your heart. Just because something makes sense from a logical perspective doesn't mean it makes sense from your heart's point of view. You have to be honest with yourself about where your heart is.

Face the truth about where you've come from, where you are now, and where you're going. Be honest about your thoughts and feelings. Honestly assess the challenges before you. What will you have to give up in order to get what you really want? Remember, in baseball terms, you can't steal second base with one foot on first. You may have to let go of what you're holding onto, even if that includes security, in order to have the freedom to grasp what you really want. In order to get what you really want out of life, you must weigh the value of what you're experiencing now against what you *could* be experiencing if you got what you really wanted. Make a decision, and then go for it.

No one will ever achieve your dreams for you. Why do you think heroes have the admiration of everyone around them? What they achieve comes at great cost. Most people aren't willing to do what it takes to get there, but we respect those who do. The only formula for success is massive, creative, and innovative energy focused on a single objective. Achieving your dreams requires all the resources you have and all those that you can imagine. Being true to yourself may require that you change the course you're on. But changing the course you're on requires one thing first — a decision. The decision behind the decision is to accept the fact that your current patterns of behavior are not yielding the results you want. The decision behind the decision is to vow to try something different — anything, as long as it is different. Only you can make this decision. Until you're willing to do so, you can expect the same results you've been getting.

How do you make the decision to stop doing what you've

always done? How do you muster the courage and the energy to alter your course? Our old habits and routines seem to hold us down like a heavy anchor. Realize that a huge ocean-liner can't turn on a dime. It takes time, patience, and a deliberate change of the forces propelling the ship in order to alter its course. Once these forces have been mobilized, the course of a ship can be changed. Once the direction of the ship is changed, even by only a few degrees, the final destination is permanently altered. Similarly, if you make "baby step" decisions to alter little things in your life, then ultimately, your whole life will change.

You don't have to wait for some crisis to erupt in your life before you decide to change. Today, you can make an internal decision that things are going to be different from now on — that you are not going to keep doing things the same old way. Lance Armstrong said, "There aren't many clearly marked, sign-post moments in your life, but occasionally they come along, and you have a choice. You can either do something the same old way, or you can make a better decision. You have to be able to recognize the moment, and to act on it, at risk of saying later, 'That's when it all could have been different.' If you're willing to make a harder choice, you can redesign your life."

Changing your life from what it is now to what you want it to be requires deliberate action. Nothing good happens to us by accident. You must *make* it happen.

Being honest about the facts and being true to yourself will change the way you make decisions. Remember, when you start looking in places you never looked before, you will start seeing things you've never seen before.

FIFTH LAW OF CRITICAL FOCUS™:
We tend to filter out what we're not expecting to see.

HEROES SEE FROM AN ELEVATED POSITION

SIXTH LAW OF CRITICAL FOCUS™:
The more we see, the more options are available to us.

The more we are able to see with our physical eyes, the more information can be transmitted to our brains. The more information our brains have, the more options we can consider. The more options we have to consider, the better our decisions become.

From the beginning, humans have been on a constant quest to increase the information available to them in order to make better decisions. Early on, we discovered that we could see more when we were standing on a mountaintop than when we were standing in the flatland or in the valley. The higher our elevation, the greater the amount of information available to us.

As primitive man, all we could do was climb, hike or crawl to the highest point in order to look for herds of animals and keep a watch out for our enemies. But as time moved on, so did man's ability to elevate himself to a higher position from which to view situations and problems. For example, during the Civil War, military officers discovered they could use hot-air balloons to elevate themselves above the battle scene in order to see the enemy positions. This new perspective changed the way they mapped strategies and made battle-field decisions. This demonstrates the Sixth Law of Critical Focus™: *The more we see, the more options are available to us.* As technology has advanced, so has our ability to "elevate" our vision and increase the information available to us. Today, we are able to see the entire world from outer space through the power of satellites.

Similarly, when you are grappling with any difficult situation, it helps to step back from the situation. It helps to elevate yourself to a higher state of mind.

Heroes see opportunities that others don't see because they see the world from an elevated position. What will you be able to see when you learn to see through heroes' eyes? Heroes see new solutions to old problems. Heroes see alternate routes to their goals when others see only dead ends.

Anthony Robbins, author of *Unlimited Power,* tells an interesting story about Colonel Sanders before he became famous. When Colonel Sanders was 65 years old, he was flat broke. This was the time in his life when he should have been retired and living off a pension or the proceeds from his investments. But this was not the case. All he had was a monthly social security check for a meager $105. This was the wrong time in his life to have a crisis. The highway that used to run near his restaurant had been re-routed and his business had gone down the tubes. All he had left was a "pretty good" recipe for fried chicken. Think about it — a recipe for fried chicken! Does this sound like what you would hang your hopes and dreams on? But he took what little he had and pursued it with all of his passion. He took his idea on the road. His grandiose idea was to sell his chick-en recipe and show people how to cook their chicken in exchange for a percentage of their profits. He would dress up in a white Southern colonial suit and drive from restaurant to restaurant trying to sell his chicken recipe. He had to sleep in his car many nights because he couldn't afford a hotel room. What would your reaction have been when you saw an old geezer in a white colonial suit walking through your door? Is it Halloween? He was turned down 1,009 times. But eventually someone finally said yes. Then another person said yes and then another. The rest is history.

Was it the Colonel's chicken recipe that made him a success? No. He had that recipe all along. It was the way he *chose* to open his eyes and *see new* ways to make money with it. Did his crisis situation *force* him to open his eyes? No. At that age, he could have just decided that life was over and started relying on friends, relatives, or the government. His eyes were opened because he made a deliberate decision not to give up. When we *choose* to keep going no matter what, life has a way of celebrating our decision by meeting us halfway. New opportunities seem to materialize out of thin air. Things we never saw before spring to life.

The Colonel did not become wealthy and famous because he was destined to become wealthy and famous. He became a hero because he *saw* what no one else saw. He made some tough decisions and created his own destiny along the way. He *decided* to follow his dream. And then he *kept deciding* every day to keep getting up and to continue pursuing his dream, even when he was tired and discouraged. He kept making these tough decisions every day, even when it seemed that the whole world was sending him a message: "This is a stupid idea." Do you have the guts to make these daily decisions in the face of extreme adversity?

Can you see through heroes' eyes well enough to walk where heroes walk?

Millions of good ideas are floating around out there. You may have some of your own. But what will make them ultimately succeed is your absolute determination to keep trying and a daily decision to keep working until you get what you want. Sheer desire and persistence makes us or breaks us.

The Colonel was not on a time clock that told him when he was "washed up." He started a whole new career, moreover a whole new industry, when society and the federal government told him it was time to retire. This is proof that the only limits are in our minds. There's no deadline for pursuing or achieving our dreams. There's no single exclusive way to do it. Whatever works for you, pursue it. If the road you're on isn't taking you toward your goals, don't give up on your goals. Try another road.

Captain Oliver Hazard Perry is another hero who saw alternate paths where others saw only dead ends. In the War of 1812, we were losing badly to the British. But a decisive battle at Lake Erie would turn the war around. At the Battle of Lake Erie, Captain Oliver Hazard Perry was a 27-year-old young man whose assignment was to break the British stronghold in the Northwest. As he sailed his ship, the *Lawrence*, into battle, the fellow American captain who was supposed to be at his side captaining the *Niagra* backed off. The British pounded the *Lawrence* mercilessly until it was badly crippled and had nothing left to give. Four-fifths of the sailors on the *Lawrence* were dead. But, the *Lawrence* bore a flag with the famous words "Don't give up the ship!" that had been uttered a few months earlier by Captain James

Lawrence with his dying breath during a battle in the Boston Harbor.

The little-known truth behind the story is that when Captain Perry's ship was of no more use to him, he did abandon that ship. He jumped aboard a small open boat and made his way under intense enemy fire to the *Niagra*, which was still unharmed. He persuaded the captain of the *Niagra* to give him control of the ship. The British ships had already been pounded in the battle with the *Lawrence*, and now they were facing the fresh and fully armed *Niagra*. It took only fifteen minutes of pounding by the *Niagra* for the British to surrender. Perry had defeated the British fleet and was now in control of all of Lake Erie. The hidden lesson behind the story is don't give up the goal, even if you have to give up the ship. Heroes become heroes because they are able to see more than one way to accomplish their dreams.

In military terms, "retreat" doesn't mean "defeat." It means to regroup and rethink in order to attack again, perhaps from a different angle or by using a different strategy. Similarly, in your life sometimes you need a "retreat."

I guess it's kind of like when your computer freezes up and all you can do is turn it off and then turn it back on again. I don't know why it works, but it does. I often think, "Maybe the computer just needed a break." My high-tech friends just laugh.

When you're refreshed, your mind thinks more clearly. You see creative solutions you hadn't previously seen. Then you can rejoin the battle with a new mindset and renewed vigor. Sometimes, you just need to "re-boot" yourself. If it works for a computer, can it work for you? Have you thought about turning your mind "off" for a few days?

In addition, in trying to decide whether to continue pursuing a certain course of action, beware of the illusion of "sunk costs." Once you have a lot of time, money, and energy invested into a project, a relationship, or a course of action, pride alone may make you reluctant to walk away from it. Business managers and investors sometimes become so wedded to a course of action that they're not able to see the hard evidence staring them in the face that they made the wrong decision. Their pride makes them blind to reality. It's hard for them to admit they may have made a mistake. They get caught in a trap because they made a decision to follow a certain course of action to which the company has now committed thousands or millions of dollars and they're now unable to admit it was a mistake. They often make matters worse by trying to rescue a dying project. Our country's involvement in the Vietnam War is another example of this phenomenon. Sometimes it's best to just pull out.

Similarly, in our personal lives sometimes we have trouble realizing we've been putting our time and energies in the wrong place. Climbing the ladder of success isn't very useful if you find out at the top that your ladder was leaning against the wrong wall.

Every now and then, it's good to stop and listen to your heart. Sometimes it is good to examine the hard evidence and messages that life may be trying to send you. Heroes pause every now and then to reassess a course of action and make whatever modifications or alterations are necessary. Sometimes it's wise to abandon a certain course of action and start over, to cut your losses and stop "throwing good money after bad."

At some point during the California Gold Rush, someone figured out that the best way to find gold was to provide goods and services to everyone else who was looking for it. Even when the gold seekers weren't finding any gold, they still needed food to eat, tools to work with, and a place to sleep. They usually paid with gold dust or gold nuggets. No matter who found the gold or where they found it, it eventually went to the merchants. The merchants kept making money during the good times and bad. The merchants kept collecting it until they had their own huge mountain of gold. There's always more than one path to your dreams. Through creativity, persistence, and patience, you *can* ultimately achieve your goal.

There is a big difference between persistence, stubbornness, determination, and *creative* persistence, *creative* stubbornness, and *creative* determination. Blind persistence is lunacy. Creative persistence is genius.

The story of Soichiro Honda is an example of creative genius at work. Upon graduating from middle school in 1922, Soichiro traveled to Tokyo with his father to respond to a help wanted ad at an automobile repair shop called Art Shokai. Soichiro was accepted as an apprentice at the shop. However, he became frustrated because his job only involved menial tasks such as cleaning up and babysitting the owner's child. When he could, he watched with fascination as the auto mechanics did their jobs. He would sneak into the shop after hours just to touch the cars.

In 1923, a great earthquake called Kanto struck Tokyo and killed nearly 100,000 people. The automobile repair shop was almost completely destroyed, along with Soichiro's dreams. But because of the earthquake, most of the mechanics quit their jobs to go spend their time helping their families rebuild. This left an opportunity for Soichiro to become a mechanic. The owner built a new temporary shop in the suburbs and began repairing cars that had been damaged in the earthquake, using Soichiro as one of his chief mechanics. Together, they bought damaged cars, fixed them up, and resold them.

At the age of 21, Soichiro opened his own automotive shop with only one employee. At first business was slow, but it began to build and within one year it began to flourish. Then another tragedy struck. A severe depression that would eventually cloak the entire world in a dark cloud began in 1929. But, because of Soichiro's excellent skills and knowledge of foreign cars, his business survived and prospered in the midst of adversity. His business grew to the point of having 15 employees.

Because of the Kanto earthquake, Soichiro understood the need to make parts that would be stronger and more durable. Soichoro saw a new solution to an old problem. He invented cast iron spokes to replace the old wooden ones. The cast iron spokes were highly celebrated at the National Industrial Exhibit and Soichiro began exporting them to other countries.

A few years later, Soichiro started making piston rings for cars. His goal was to design a piston ring that would be acceptable to the very young Toyota Corporation, and become a mass production supplier to Toyota. But he was having trouble coming up with a piston ring that could be mass produced. The problem was in the composition of the metal. It looked like another dead end. *But heroes see alternate paths to their dreams.* Knowing that he could not rely on his middle school education any longer, he consulted with Professor Takashi Tashiro at the Hamamatsu Technical School. Then, at the age of 30, Soichiro enrolled in a technical high school to learn metallurgy. The teenagers that surrounded him at the high school stared at him and laughed, but Soichiro was oblivious to them. Soichoro did not bother to take the graduation exams. Upon being informed that he would not receive a graduation diploma, Soichiro retorted that a diploma was worth less than a movie theater ticket. "A ticket guarantees that you can get into the theater. But a diploma doesn't guarantee that you can make a living."

In 1936, he built a racecar with his brother Benjiro, using an old airplane engine and handmade parts. But the car crashed during a race, causing Soichoro a broken shoulder and severe facial injuries. Now he was seriously injured, his savings were gone, and the piston ring business was failing. But Soichiro did not see a brick wall. Instead, he kept trying to come up with a piston ring that Toyota would buy. He took fifty of his best piston rings out of a group of 30,000 to try to sell them to Toyota. He was struggling financially and he even had to pawn his young wife's jewelry to make ends meet. Can you imagine your spouse's reaction if *you* pawned their most prized possession? Toyota rejected his proposal because only three of the fifty piston rings passed inspection. It was another dead end. He abandoned that business and went to work for another small automotive company so he could have a steady paycheck.

While at the new company, Soichiro invented a piston ring polishing machine. It was revolutionary and simple to operate. After three long years of trial and error, his *creative* persistence paid off and now he was making excellent piston rings.

In 1942, the company he worked for was acquired by Toyota. Toyota was now finally using the piston rings that he had designed. Soichiro eventually became the Executive Director of the company. The factory produced military supplies, with the piston rings going into military aircraft and ships. During this time, Soichiro also designed metal propellers to replace the old wooden ones. Soichiro also invented an automatic propeller-cutting machine, which reduced the time needed to make a propeller from one week to fifteen minutes.

In 1945, the plant was destroyed by a U.S. air raid along with most of the city it was in. It looked like another dead end. But Soichiro saw what others around him did not see. He collected the metal from leftover military vehicles and airplanes, moved to a new city to open a small factory, and continued production on a small scale. Finally, the end of the war brought an end to his piston ring production business. Dead end again.

Tokyo and most industrial cities had been destroyed in the war. Fields had been burned and almost all of Japan was in disarray. There was an extreme shortage of goods and food. There was very little transportation. Gasoline was rationed and sometimes impossible to find. Soichiro couldn't even get enough gasoline to drive his car into town to buy food for his family. The buses and trains were so crowded that people had to crawl in and out of the windows.

But he was a true hero. Again, he saw what others could not see. In 1946, Soichiro realized that what people needed was a cheap and quick way to get around town. He took regular bicycles and installed small engines on them, which were left over from the war. They were about the size of a lawnmower engine. But he soon ran out of military surplus engines. Another dead end.

Did this stop Soichiro? No. He decided to start making his own small engines. However, there was one small problem — he had no money. So he wrote letters to bicycle shop owners throughout Japan, explaining his idea to make motorbikes and asking them to invest. With the money that a few of them invested, he started manufacturing his own engines and motorbikes. The first motorbikes he made were too big and bulky, and very few Japanese bought them. Dead end again.

But, like a smart bomb, Soichiro listened to the feedback and adjusted accordingly. Soichiro changed his approach. He stripped his motor bike down and made it much lighter. The new design won the Emperor's Award. In time, this little motorbike captured 60% of the Japanese market and Soichiro began exporting them to Taiwan.

In 1948, Soichiro established the Honda Motor Company. By 1949, Honda's production of motorbikes was up to 1,000 units per month. Also during that year, Honda designed a 2-stroke, 98cc engine and thus, the first lightweight motorcycle was born. By 1951, Honda had 150 employees and annual sales of 330 million yen. A year later, the number of employees had increased to 1,300 and sales reached 2,438 million yen per year.

But at the end of the Korean War, a major recession hit the economy and it became impossible for Honda to pay for the manufacturing equipment that he needed. Would his company go under? No. He borrowed money from the

Mitsubishi Bank and his business was saved.

In 1959, Soichiro started the American Honda Motor Company. By the early 1960s Honda had expanded his business and was making small four-wheeled vehicles. Honda's S800 model was exhibited at automobile shows in Europe where it received very high praise.

In the 1970s America went through a fuel shortage and consumers were looking for alternatives to the giant gas guzzlers made by the American manufacturers. The Honda Civic and the Honda Accord were the answer. By the 1980s, the Honda Motor Company was one of the largest automotive companies in the world. Soichiro Honda is an example of how heroes see alternative paths to their goals when others see only dead ends.

Heroes also see new solutions to old problems that others do not see. In 1903, J.L. Kraft began selling cheese in the back of a horse-drawn wagon. But back then, cheese molded or dried out quickly so there was a tremendous amount of waste. It was a problem that people had dealt with for hundreds of years. There seemed to be no answer to the problem. Another problem was that the cheese also varied in texture and taste from batch to batch. J.L. Kraft experimented over and over and finally developed a process that would give the cheese a consistent texture and taste throughout. He also came up with a way to wrap the cheese in foil or in airtight plastic. This solved the drying out and molding problems. As a result of these innovations, J.L. Kraft's humble cheese business began to grow and became one of the largest cheese manufacturers in America. By 1925, Kraft was exporting his cheese all over Canada, England, Germany, Australia, India, and Asia.

In the 1930's the same depression that was sweeping the world hit America. Businesses were failing left and right. Business executives were committing suicide and people were standing in soup lines so they could eat. But Kraft had an idea. He came up with a new type of dressing called Miracle Whip, which was a blend of traditional mayonnaise, salad dressing, and twenty different spices. It was inexpensive to produce and it had a wonderful flavor that could be used to accent fruit, vegetables, and salads. Some say that it was called Miracle Whip because it was the miracle that allowed Kraft to survive and prosper during the depression while other business collapsed. In time, Kraft would come up with even more innovative products such as Velveeta, Cheez Whiz, and Kraft Macaroni and Cheese, which are loved by kids the world over.

Heroes become heroes because they learn to see from an elevated position. This allows them to see new answers to old problems, and alternative paths instead of dead ends. What will you begin to see when you learn to see through the eyes of heroes?

SIXTH LAW OF CRITICALFOCUS™:
**The more we see,
the more options are available to us.**

HEROES FOCUS ON THE PURPOSE ON THE OTHER SIDE OF PAIN

SEVENTH LAW OF CRITICAL FOCUS™:
*We have the power to choose what to focus on
no matter what is going on in the world around us.*

One Thanksgiving, Eleanor Roosevelt was serving food at a local soup kitchen. More street people showed up than anticipated. They were running out of food and worried that not everyone would get to eat. As Eleanor was delivering two plates of food, her thumbs slipped into the gravy on the plates. The gravy was extremely hot. Her natural reaction was to drop the plates instantly, but she knew that if she did so, two people would go without their Thanksgiving dinner. So she held on. She made a decision that someone else's Thanksgiving was more important than her desire to avoid the pain. She found meaning in her temporary suffering and decided to keep going. In that split second, she *chose* where to put her focus. Someone else's happiness was more important than her temporary pain. Heroes *choose* to focus on the purpose on the other side of pain.

When you are facing what looks like insurmountable odds, how do you know when it is time to quit or keep going? In the timeless movie *It's a Wonderful Life*, George Bailey suddenly encounters financial, legal, and business trouble the likes of which he has never seen. He's faced with going to jail for a crime he didn't commit and not being able to support his family. The odds against him seem insurmountable. He sees no way out for himself or his family. He's desperate. He begins to wish he had never been born. He feels that everything he has worked for all of his life has been lost and that there is nothing he can do to regain it.

He's about to commit suicide when an angel intervenes. The angel shows him what life would have been like in his hometown had he never been born. The people he had helped throughout his life went without help because he wasn't there. His brother died as a child because George wasn't there to save him. Hundreds of men on a transport ship died because his brother in turn wasn't there to save them. A pharmacist became an alcoholic and a street person because George wasn't there as a teen to correct an error the pharmacist made in a prescription, and the customer died as a result. The unscrupulous Mr. Potter became the most powerful man in town, abusing and taking advantage of many people. The evil influences in George Bailey's hometown that he counter-balanced with his life went unchecked without his presence. His wife never married and became an old maid.

In the movie, George Bailey begins to see the value that his life has brought to all those around him — despite his current troubles. He wishes he were alive again, if only just for them. He begs the angel to bring things back to the way they were when he was alive. Then, in an instant, the angel brings him back to reality. In the end of the movie, all the people whom George has helped throughout his life come to his aid in his greatest hour of need and give him just what he needs to survive his crisis. One moment, the world seems bleak, but in the next, his perspective shifts from his own troubles to the troubles of those around him whom he was able to help. This gives him hope and a reason to keep living that is bigger than his problems. This feeling of purposefulness becomes the ray of sunshine that gives him a reason to keep living.

It's a moving story, and in the end, George Bailey realizes that all of the good he has done and all the good he has left to do in life outweigh whatever pain he is experiencing due to his current problems. He realizes that the significance of his life isn't in how pleasant and stress-free his own life is, but in the value he brings to the lives of those around him. Yet, when George made his decision *not* to commit suicide, his horrible situation hadn't yet changed. The only thing that changed was what he *chose* to focus on. Once his *focus* changed, he came to believe that his life had significance and a purpose. Once he was looking at the situation from the top of the mountain, he saw everything in a whole new light. Now he was looking through heroes' eyes.

From what position are you viewing your situation? Is it from the mountaintop or the valley floor? What have you *chosen* to focus on?

Whatever your situation, before you can decide whether to quit or keep going, you've got to decide how important it is for you to accomplish your goal. Viktor Frankl, survivor of a Nazi death camp, says that above all, the thing that kept him going was the thought that the world needed what he had to offer when he got out. He had an unfinished book that he needed to write. So, he *chose* to focus on that one small purpose despite what was going on the world around him. Frankl explained that those in the camp who focused on what little the world had left to offer them were most likely to be found dead on their bunks in the morning or to "throw themselves against the fence" in order to end it all. He said one could always tell when people had given up hope by the look in their eyes and the way they walked. Then you knew it was just a matter of time.

> *"In some ways, suffering ceases to be suffering*
> *at the moment it finds a meaning."*
> — Viktor Frankl

The people who survived the death camps tended to *focus* on a specific purpose or on the person who was waiting for them when they got out. They *focused* on the ray of sunlight they had to offer the world — not on what the world had, or did not have, to offer them. This demonstrates the Seventh Law of Critical Focus™. *We have the power to choose what to focus on, no matter what is going on in the world around us.* This requires a vivid imagination and lots of creativity. But you can deliberately *choose* to use your imagination just as Frankl did. This is the decision behind the decision.

When we feel like people expect great things from us, we experience a sense of purpose. We sit up tall. We feel a sense of mission. If you felt there was something important that the world needed you to accomplish before you died, wouldn't you work as hard as you could to get it done in order to fulfill your destiny? Suddenly, whatever you're going through seems to find purpose and meaning. You want to keep going no matter what. You feel strong and satisfied.

Happiness does not automatically come from the elimination of pain. Viktor Frankl, in his book *Man's Search for Meaning*, and the Dalai Lama, in his book *The Art of Happiness*, both teach us not to confuse pleasure with happiness. Pleasure relies on the physical senses and can look a lot like happiness. But happiness relies on the spiritual senses and requires a belief that you have a mission, a purpose, or some significance in the universe. If you have this firm and unwavering belief, even physical hardship and suffering cannot take away your satisfaction with life. Happiness, therefore, does not come from the elimination of pain, but from the realization of purpose.

> *"Man's main concern is not to gain pleasure or to avoid pain, but rather to see a meaning in his life. That is why man is even ready to suffer, on the condition, to be sure, that his suffering has meaning."*
>
> — VIKTOR FRANKL

You don't have to wait for an angel to speak to you in a vision or a dream to give you a mission. You have the option to *choose* to believe that there is something worth accomplishing on the other side of your current struggle. But this is a conscious, deliberate choice, not an accident or a result of divine inspiration.

In his book, *Every Second Counts*, Lance Armstrong sums it up this way: "If I were religious, I'd say cancer advocacy is what God would like me to do, but I'm not. So, I'll simply say that's what I have the opportunity to do, and what I'm designed to do." Lance Armstrong became a cancer advocate not because of divine inspiration, but because one day he *decided* it was a worthwhile purpose to give his life to. A hero makes a conscious decision to *focus* on the purpose on the other side of the pain. This is what he sees and this vision keeps him going.

You can *choose* a specific purpose and then *choose* to give your life to it or you can continue living your life as is. Have you ever stopped and made a list of things you'd like to do for the sake of humanity before you die? What if money and time were not obstacles? Now what would you do? Make a list. Now ask yourself, "What's the tiniest of baby steps I can take this month toward accomplishing this dream?" Now go out and take that baby step. Or at least start to crawl.

"We are not humans having a spiritual experience,
we are spiritual beings having a human experience."
— TEILHARD DE CHARDIN

How do heroes change their focus when they are suffering extreme pain or difficulty? They use the power of their imagination. Your imagination alone can help you get past any difficult situation you are facing. When we don't exercise the power of our imagination, all we can see is our current struggle, which causes fear and depression. This fear steals our energy and takes away the motivation that we need to get us through to the other side. In contrast, using your imagination to focus on specific, positive pictures gives birth to hope, faith, and courage. But, you have to make a conscious *choice* to create these pictures. Then you have to make a conscious choice to focus on them. Then you have to make a deliberate choice to believe. When you choose to believe, excitement and energy follow. Feelings follow faith and not the other way around. If you are focusing on how you feel right now and waiting for that to change before you choose to believe, it is like waiting for your fever to go away before you take the medicine.

If we *believe* the costs are too high or the possibility of success is too low, we may become discouraged and refuse to act at all. When you refuse to act, you create a self-fulfilling prophecy that prevents you from achieving your goals. Our beliefs and perceptions (the visions in our head) alone have the ability to either inspire and motivate us or defeat us before we ever get started.

Have you ever sat in traffic behind someone who was trying to decide whether it's safe to merge into traffic? From where you sit, it may look like a 747 airplane could have merged by now. Their decision to wait for a bigger opening is based on their own perception of the traffic and lack of confidence in their own ability or the ability of their car to thread the gap. They don't move because they *believe* they can't make it, whereas if they thought they *could* make it, they would go. Sometimes you just want to kick them in the pants and yell, "Go for it!" or some other expletive. Similarly, our *beliefs* can limit our actions or spur us into action. Sometimes what we need is a good kick in the pants and to hear someone yell, "Go for it!"

When my father got his real estate license, it was during a severe recession in Texas. To make matters worse, the prevailing interest rate on home mortgages was a shocking

18%! His timing for entering this profession wasn't perfect, but his enthusiasm more than made up for it. His excitement and desire to succeed made him oblivious to the obstacles. His company repeatedly gave him awards for being in the Million Dollar Club. One day, another realtor, reading the newspaper with his feet propped up on his desk, caught my father on his way to an appointment with a client. Looking up from his newspaper, he said, "Hey, what do you think you're doing? Don't you know no one is buying? We're in a recession!"

My father looked at him blankly and in his innocence said, "Well . . . no one told me about it," and he walked right out the door and kept selling. Remember, many of life's problems aren't caused by *what* we see, but by *how* we see.

The world-famous Italian violinist Niccolo Paganini (1782–1840) was playing before a large audience when a string on his violin broke. He improvised beautifully and continued to play. Then another string broke. Then another. Soon, he had only one string left. Paganini continued to improvise and completed the entire composition with just one string. When the applause finally died down, the conductor turned to the audience and shouted, "Paganini . . . and one string!" The audience roared and Paganini began playing again on that one string. It is amazing what we can accomplish when we have already decided that nothing can stand in our way. This is the decision behind the decision.

If our *belief* is that the goal is so important and exciting that it's worth pursuing at any cost, then our *belief* alone launches us into action, and nothing can stop us. This massive action alone, coupled with an undying belief in the goal, prevents us from ever giving up. Tenacity and time are often enough to make our dreams come true. You can create your own self-fulfilling prophecy if your *belief* is strong enough to get yourself off the couch. But this requires that you *choose* to exercise the power of your imagination and focus on what you see with your mind.

How strong is the power of imagination? Maxwell Maltz explained in his book *Psycho-Cybernetics* that experimental and clinical psychologists have established beyond a doubt that the brain cannot distinguish between an actual experience and one that we've only imagined. In one well-known clinical experiment, behavioral scientists concluded that *visualizing* throwing a basketball through the hoop is more effective at improving scoring than actually *practicing* throwing it through the hoop. In the experiment, one group of basketball players was allowed to practice throwing the basketball through the hoop. The other group was only allowed to visualize throwing the basketball through the hoop without physically doing it. In the final test, the second group far outscored the first. What does this tell you about the power of visualization?

If it can help you score more baskets, can visualization help you accomplish your goals and dreams in real life? You be the judge.

While in the death camp, Viktor Frankl frequently closed his eyes and visually transported himself to a classroom where he was a professor, teaching bright young students who were eager to hear what he had to say. He focused his attention on the good he had to offer the world and momentarily shut out the bad things around him. His imagination became his reality during that otherwise dark time. He used this powerful visualization process to remove himself from his circumstances and give himself hope and a reason to endure. His vivid imagination was his grappling hook that gave him something to hold onto in the future and kept him alive.

Several years after he was liberated, Frankl found himself teaching eager young students, just as he had visualized. This was no accident. It was not fate. It was not the fulfillment of a divine prophecy. It was the result of a conscious, deliberate *choice* that Frankl made to escape his circumstances through the power of his imagination while people all around him saw only suffering and despair. What Frankl saw made all the difference.

Similarly, Lance Armstrong used the power of imagination to help him get through the torturous process of chemotherapy. In *Every Second Counts*, Armstrong explains:

"You can alter any experience with your mind — it's up to you to determine what the quality of each moment is. *Concentration* and *belief* can make even chemo, no matter how sickening it is, a positive experience. It takes practice, but it's possible. I used to tell myself when I threw up or when it burned so badly to urinate, that the sensations represented the cancer leaving my body. I was pissing it out, puking it out, coughing it out."

Heroes *choose* what they focus on despite what is going on in the world around them. Are you focusing only on what you see with your physical eyes or on what you can see with the eyes of your imagination? It could be that all of your hard work up to this point is about to pay off. Who knows, the very next thing you're about to try may put you over the hump. But you'll never know unless you keep trying. There's hope. There is always hope.

> *"The mind is its own place, and in itself*
> *can make a heav'n of hell and a hell of heav'n."*
> — JOHN MILTON

Belief is the most powerful generator of energy and strength in our lives. There is not a single technological achievement that humans have accomplished without the power of belief. Humans could not have achieved one positive thing in history without the power of belief. This is because belief is what drives us to act.

Belief drives us to experiment and to keep experimenting until we find something that works. Belief is what drives us to seek out something better than what we are experiencing. Belief is what drove the first explorer's ships around the world. Belief is what propelled our rockets to the moon and beyond.

Belief in a concept or idea is more powerful than the greatest weapon ever created and stronger than all the armies in the world. An *undying* belief in a single concept or idea can stop an army dead in its tracks and make it turn around. Need an example?

In the early years of Christianity, it was the Romans who tortured and killed the Christians. But in time, the Romans would become the chief messengers and enforcers of this faith, even to the point of torturing and killing those who opposed it. No army in the world could have forced the Romans to stop killing Christians. No army in the world could have forced the Romans to adopt Christianity. It was the undying belief in an idea by a small group of people that, over time, made this change. It was the belief in this idea that changed the history of the world. The same can be said of the beliefs held by Muhammad, Confucius, and Mahatma Gandhi. Belief is the single most powerful force in the universe. Fire cannot burn it. Water cannot drown it. The most sophisticated weapons ever invented are powerless against it. If belief can change the history of the world, can it change the course of your life?

Belief is what makes us think there might actually be a purpose for our existence.

But, you have to make a conscious *choice* to believe. It doesn't happen by accident. Belief is the gas that powers your engine. But, every now and then, you've got to stop for more gas. The *positive* visions in your head are the gas. You get to *choose* whether to exercise the power of your imagination no matter what is going on in the physical world around you. If you are having trouble coming up with your own positive mental images to focus on, there are thousands of seminars, books, workshops, preachers, and motivational speakers available to help you.

> *"Faith is the substance of things hoped for,*
> *the evidence of things not seen."*
> — HEBREWS 11:1

I once heard a story of a doctor and a pharmacist who had experimented for years with recipes for a soft drink. Eventually, the doctor gave up and sold his interest to the pharmacist. The pharmacist continued, and just a few weeks later he developed the formula for Coca Cola, the most widely sold soft drink in the world today. The pharmacist's name was Dr. John S. Pemberton. The year was 1886.

During the gold rush days in Colorado, a man named R.U. Darby and his uncle went west in search of gold. With only a pick and a shovel, they dug and dug until they finally struck the shiny gold ore. But they needed specialized machinery to bring the gold to the surface. They quietly buried their small mine and went back east to Williamsburg, Maryland, and told a few relatives and neighbors of their find. They convinced them to invest and loan them the money they needed to buy the equipment and have it shipped to the mine.

They brought up the first car of ore and shipped it to the smelter. The results showed that they had one of the richest mines ever found in Colorado. A few more cars of this gold would pay their debts and then they could start reaping enormous profits. But then tragedy struck. The vein of gold disappeared. They searched and searched — desperate to pick up the vein of gold again. But no luck. They continued drilling in vain and after a few more weeks of frustration, they gave up. They sold the machinery to a junk man for a few hundred dollars and took the train back home.

In the meantime, the junk man called a mining engineer to look at the mine. The engineer took some calculations and concluded that the project had failed because the owners were not familiar with "fault lines." The junk man took over the drilling and found the vein of gold *within three feet* of where the Darbys had stopped drilling! The mine turned out to be one of the biggest gold mines ever discovered in Colorado.

*"Many of life's failures are people who did not realize
how close they were to success when they gave up."*

— THOMAS EDISON

When you quit, you create a permanent solution to a temporary problem. When you quit, you guarantee the result you fear most — that you won't succeed. The fact is, when you quit, you will not be around to experience the success that makes all your suffering count for something. Turn your pain into a purpose. Remember, the world is counting on you to do what only you can do.

Consider the development of fiber optics, which has allowed people all over the world to communicate with each other at the speed of light. After two years and millions of dollars, late one evening, after everyone had left the laboratory, a scientist named Donald Keck decided to try shining a laser beam through yet one more sample of glass fiber drawn out as thin as a hair. Bending over a microscope, he slowly began to align the helium neon laser with the fiber's core. On every previous attempt, the signal-carrying light pulses had quickly disappeared. But not on this night. All of the sudden, the light raced all the way along the glass, bounced off the far end, and sailed right back. Keck rushed out into the hall and caught his research chief at the elevator. "Hey, you want to see something neat?" he asked. And that was the advent of fiber optic communication lines, which would revolutionize the telecommunications industry.

Now fiber optics are used to transmit voice, video, and computer data at laser-pulse speed across the world. It would have been easy to quit after spending so much time and money and continually coming up with nothing. But

Donald Keck persevered. He kept trying various alternatives until he found one that worked. He made a decision not to quit.

> *"There is no pain in the wound*
> *received in the moment of victory."*
> — PUBLIUS SYRUS

Dr. Gerald Mann, pastor of Riverbend Church in Austin, Texas, tells a story of a very successful businessman who called him one night in desperation. He was a devoted family man who had started a small business and built it into a corporate empire. He had given liberally over the years to charities and to his employees in the form of stock options. He said he was about to be indicted for tax fraud the next day. He knew he was innocent. But he couldn't stand the shame, heartache, and emotional turmoil the indictment would bring to his family and himself, not to mention the thousands of dollars in attorney's fees required to defend himself. He had a gun in his hand and was about to commit suicide. Dr. Mann tried to counsel him, but the man lost patience and was about to hang up. He had already made up his mind to *focus* on the worst case scenario. What he was focusing on determined what he *believed.* This belief caused him to discount what Dr. Mann was saying.

The last thing Dr. Mann uttered quickly before the phone went dead was, "Wait to worry! Wait until they indict you. Wait till you get a lawyer. Then wait till you get his bill. Wait till you're pronounced guilty. Wait for the sentencing. Wait for the cell door to close. But wait to worry."

Sure enough, the man was indicted. He paid thousands of dollars in legal fees, but two years later he was acquitted of all charges.

Some time later, at a fundraiser, the man saw Dr. Mann across the room, ran up to him and said, "I want you to know that your three words saved my life. I have them posted everywhere. In my car, on the refrigerator, on my desk. All over the offices. What I've learned is that God is out there in the future waiting for us." The few words Gerald Mann squeezed in that day were all the man needed to help him *change his focus.* Once he changed his focus, he was able to believe something different than what he had previously believed. If the man had actually taken his life that night, he wouldn't have been around to see his name cleared. Similarly, in our own lives, we don't know if we will succeed until the end of the story, when all the facts have unfolded. God's delays are not God's denials. *Wait to worry.* God is out there in the future waiting for us.

"Now and then I go about pitying myself and all the while my soul is being blown by great winds across the sky."
— Ojibway Native American proverb

The story told by Dr. Mann raises a very important issue. More people have contemplated suicide than would ever admit to it. If you are contemplating this option, please read the rest of this chapter carefully. If you know someone who's dealing with this issue, share this chapter with them.

If you've ever seriously contemplated suicide, what you're saying is that you're tired of fighting and struggling against the odds with no results. So you justify your desire to quit by *choosing* to believe there is no hope. But there is *always* hope. You just have to open your eyes and learn to see through the eyes of heroes. The world needs the gifts you have to give. No one can fulfill your role in life like you can. If you cash in your chips, you'll be robbing people of the gifts that *only you* can give.

"Never give in. Never. Never. Never. Never."
— Winston Churchill

Dr. Mann's story also demonstrates that other people's words have the power to change our focus. If other people's words can change our focus, isn't it possible that *our own* words can change our *own* focus? You have the power to carefully choose the words you utter to yourself. Many books have been written on this subject. You can change your focus by saying things out loud to yourself. It helps to say things out loud because otherwise, if they are mere thoughts, they get clouded and mixed up with all of your other thoughts. Your words have the power to change the course of your life by changing what you focus on.

One of the most profound phrases I've ever heard is that "misery is transient." It's never here to stay. If you are miserable and frustrated with life, it may be because you're going through a transition in your life. Transitions are tough. Transitions, by definition, mean things aren't the way they used to be, and you wonder if they'll ever be the same again. You've lost something you feel you can never replace. If the transition is painful enough, you may wonder why you should go on living. You ask yourself, "What's the point?"

The fact that you haven't seen God's provision yet means you're still in transition. In baseball terms, you're in that very tenuous place when your foot has left the safety of first base but you haven't yet reached the security of second base. The fear and anxiety you feel are normal, but this *is not a reason to quit*. It is a reason to press forward with all your heart until you get to second base. The thing about transitions is that they're temporary, even though, while you're in them, they seem like an eternity. If you just hold out long enough, you'll make it to second base.

Most women who have given birth know that the worst part of labor is what is referred to as "transition." This is the point in the delivery process where women feel the most excruciating pain they've ever experienced in their life. This is the point in the delivery process when most women scream out, demand drugs, curse their husband, and swear they can't take it anymore. This is also the last critical stage before the baby is born. When the baby is born and laid gently in the mother's arms, her tears of anguish turn into tears of joy.

> *"Whether you choose your change or not, there are unlived potentialities within you, interest and talents that you have not yet explored. Transitions clear the ground for new growth. They drop the curtain so the stage can be set for a new scene. What is it, at this point in your life, that is waiting quietly backstage for an entrance cue?"*
>
> — WILLIAM BRIDGES

Sometimes, the best and highest purpose of our life cannot be realized until we've gone through a very difficult time. But this is life's way of molding us into what we need to be in order to go into the next phase of our life. We must be molded and shaped into what we are to become. If clay had feelings, how do you think it would feel while it was being slammed down on the table, beaten, pulled in all directions, spun round and round as it was being shaped into a pot, and put into the oven where it would harden? If the clay could speak, would it curse out loud? Would it blame others? Would it try to throw itself off the table? How would you feel if you were the clay? Would you be angry at the potter? The transition process is often very painful, frustrating, and confusing. We curse out loud. We blame others. We just want to quit. But there's victory on the other side of every transition — if you *choose* to focus on it and *believe* it. There's always something better on the other side.

Consider the life of Moses. The son of Hebrew slaves, Moses was nonetheless raised in the luxurious Egyptian palace as though he were Pharaoh's own son. He had never known a day of poverty, pain, or hunger. One day he discovered that he was really the son of a Hebrew slave. He had compassion for the suffering of his fellow Hebrews. He decided to do what he could. He killed an Egyptian who was beating a Hebrew slave, and for that, he was exiled to the desert. He wandered poor, destitute, hungry, and alone until a poor shepherd family found him. He found work as a shepherd, an occupation he would normally have despised as a member of the Egyptian ruling class. Considering his previous luxuries in the palace where he had lived, Moses' life now looked bleak. Not only had he lost his wealth and prestige, but also *his own actions* had caused him to lose the very power to do what he had set out to do in the first place — liberate his own people. How do you think this made him feel? Have you ever been in a position where you knew it was your own poor judgment that caused a decision that set you back a few notches in life? How did this make you feel?

At this point in his life, Moses must have had feelings of hopelessness, depression ("I can't do anything right!"), and lack of purpose ("My life is over"). He could have been the next co-ruler of Egypt. How did he reconcile that with now being a goat herder living on the fringes of society? But it was during this transition that God was preparing him for his life's mission. He had to go through the fire in order to be refined for his best and highest use. Ultimately, he became God's tool to deliver the Hebrew people from Egyptian bondage. The victory was won because Moses endured the transition and became the man God wanted him to be. He held on long enough to see his dream fulfilled in a way he never could have imagined. He saw the delivery of not just one or two Hebrew slaves, but of all his people in one mass exodus, a people that later became the great nation of Israel.

All my life, I have heard that God makes everything, even bad things, turn out for the best. If this is true, then I wonder if God is big enough to make even our own "bad decisions" (like Moses' decision) work out for the good in the grand scheme of things. Moses' story suggests that he can. What you thought was a bad decision may turn out to be a good decision in the long run.

I believe that the significance of any series of events cannot be determined until enough time has passed and we've become who we're supposed to be. When we become who we are supposed to be, then we can see through a new set of eyes. The crux of the matter is that all the frustration, depression, and confusion you may be experiencing could be but the labor pains before your "birth." You are in transition. If you give up now, you'll never experience the birth. The decision behind the decision is to focus on the purpose on the other side of pain.

SEVENTH LAW OF CRITICAL FOCUS™:
We have the power to choose what to focus on, no matter what is going on in the world around us.

HEROES DO MORE THAN JUST FACE THEIR FEARS

"'Come to the edge,' he said.
They said, 'We are afraid.'
'Come to the edge,' he said.
They came.
He pushed them ...
And they flew."

— GUILLAUME APOLLINAIRE

Sometimes the biggest obstacle standing in our way is not the obstacle. It is our fear of the obstacle. But what causes fear? Normally, it is a physical threat to our health, our well-being, or our pocketbooks. But what about a really good horror movie? Behaviorial psychologists have concluded that it matters not whether the threat is real or one we've only imagined, the feeling of fear that we feel is the same.

Fear is merely the result of focusing on negative images, whether real or imagined. When we focus on scary things, we come to believe they *might* happen. It is this *belief* that causes an emotion we call fear. Therefore, at the most basic level, fear is caused by a belief. Sometimes what we believe is real. Sometimes it is not. But it all stems from a belief.

Sometimes our fear is so strong that we become frozen and unable to shake the negative images that are driving that fear. It becomes like a broken video image going round and round and round in our head. We can try to focus on positive images, but sometimes we just can't shake the fear.

It is during these times that the only way to conquer our fears is to close our eyes to our fears and plunge right through them. During the Civil War, a Union admiral named David Farragut led a flotilla of eighteen ships as they stormed past three Confederate forts to engage a Confederate fleet. Farragut was sixty-three years old, frail, and suffering from vertigo. He was so sick that he ordered himself lashed to the rigging of his flagship so that he could lead his men into battle. A torpedo (as mines were called back then) sank the lead ship, and the captains of the other Union vessels were terrified at the sight of other floating mines. Farragut shouted, "Damn the torpedoes; full speed ahead!" As they proceeded, the waterlogged mines bumped along the hulls of the Union ships but failed to go off. The Union ships steamed on and ultimately forced the surrender of the Confederate fleet. Heroes do more than just face their fears. They look beyond their fears and focus on the task at hand.

"Pushing through fear is less frightening than living with the underlying fear that comes from a feeling of helplessness."
— SUSAN JEFFERS

If you know what you should do and fear is the only thing holding you back, you just have to do it. You will never be able to know all the answers before you make a final decision. Nothing is 100%. Nothing is a sure thing. Everything is a calculated risk. Even standing still is a risk. When you stand still, you risk losing the benefits you would have obtained if you had moved forward. There is no neutral ground. Even by not deciding, you have made a decision.

> *"Life has a way of forcing decisions*
> *on those who vacillate."*
> — NELSON MANDELA

I remember the first time I stood on the high limestone bluffs above Lake Travis in Austin. I looked at the water below, trying to decide whether to dive in. I don't know how high it was, but to me it seemed as high as the cliffs of Acapulco. I had scaled the limestone bluff from the water in my bare feet. Now I stood at the top, about to jump in. As much as I wanted to do this, I couldn't make my body move forward. I fidgeted from side to side while I thought about it. My friends were watching, waiting, and cheering me on from a boat far below. I leaned forward and stared into the blue water. Plenty of people were diving off the cliff unharmed. Although there was no apparent reason to be afraid, I was terrified. I stood there for what seemed like an eternity. In my mind, a videotape of the impending doom replayed over and over — my mangled body smashed against the rocks hidden just beneath the surface of the water.

After awhile, I realized that the only way to do what I had come there to do was to stop thinking about it. The decision behind the decision was to change what I was watching on the TV in my mind. I forced myself to visualize a video player. Then I saw myself pressing the STOP and EJECT buttons in order to stop the scary scenes from playing. I saw the videotape pop out and the TV screen go blank. Now all I could see was the beautiful blue water and people having fun. Once I had "ejected" these scary scenes from my mind, the feeling of fear literally went away. Now the decision was easy. All I had to do was throw my body forward. Gravity would do the rest. Finally, I did it. I just jumped. I had never before jumped from a point so high that I actually had time to see things and think on the way down. But I did this time. It was exhilarating. I did it again several times. It was great.

As I look back on it today, I am amazed at how our emotions are tied to what we see in our mind's eye. If you can change the channels on the TV in your mind, you can change how you feel. If you don't believe me, try this experiment. Go rent the movie *Schindler's List* and watch the whole thing. Now write down the date and how you feel. The next day, go rent your favorite comedy and watch the whole thing. Write down the date and how you feel. Compare the two journal entries. Is there any difference in how you felt after watching each movie?

Now, think about how you feel after watching a scary movie. Do you ever find yourself walking a little faster or looking over your shoulder when you come out of the theater? Are you afraid to go to the bathroom with the lights off that night? Why is that? Is there any evidence that the scenes playing in your head drive how you feel?

The beautiful thing is that you can change the visions in your head by the force of your will, by making an internal decision. You can "eject" one movie from your head and pop another one in. But, as Lance Armstrong explained in the last chapter, this requires a deliberate decision, lots of imagination, and the sheer force of will.

A couple of years after my cliff jump, I felt the wind whipping against my face as I sat with my legs dangling outside of an open door of a *perfectly good airplane* thousands of feet above the earth. The buildings far below looked like tiny little dots. I was definitely not following those silly little safety rules they teach you when you fly somewhere. "Please put your tray tables upright and buckle your seatbelts." It was an unnerving feeling as I sat there with my legs dangling in thin air. My brain knew what to do, but my body refused to move. Then, all at once, I was airborne, free-falling thousands of feet above the lovely planet earth. What an incredible feeling! Curiously, I was not nearly as afraid to leap from that plane as I was the first time I jumped off of that cliff into Lake Travis.

> *"You gain strength and confidence by every experience in which you stop to look fear in the face. You are able to say to yourself, "I have lived through this . . . I can take the next thing that comes along." You must do the thing you think you cannot do."*
>
> — ELEANOR ROOSEVELT

In life, some decisions are just that way. Too often we become paralyzed by our own fears — fear of the unknown, fear of making the wrong decision, fear of what other people might say. So we do nothing and remain stuck where we are indefinitely, waiting for something else to move us, waiting for something to change. Inside, you know what you have to do, but you are paralyzed with fear. It is not a matter of indecisiveness. It is a matter of mustering up the courage to do it. In your mind, you play out all the scenarios of things that could go wrong. You can't get them out of your mind. These are excuses for not doing what you know you need to do. A friend of mine in Austin, Cindy Bourland, calls this the "paralysis of analysis." But at some point you have to stop thinking and command your body to take action. Once you take that first irreversible step, other forces take over. Your momentum takes you the rest of the way.

You just have to make that first internal decision to move. Some people call this a leap of faith. I just call it a leap — *a decision to act.* Whether you are fearful or not has nothing to do with it. You just act. It is during that moment that all the nervous energy generated by your thoughts and feelings is converted into the energy to act. It happens when you finally decide to sit down and write that letter or make that phone call, accept that job offer, tell someone "yes," register for that class, buy a plane ticket, fill out that application, or sign that document.

> *"When you make a choice, you mobilize vast human energies and resources which otherwise go untapped."*
> — ROBERT FRITZ

It is not always a good idea to wait for the "best" time to act. In some cases, by waiting too long we lose the only opportunity we will ever have to make a critical difference. D-Day was perhaps the most decisive military engagement of World War II. But General Dwight D. Eisenhower nearly blew D-Day because he couldn't decide the best moment for attack. Finally, he said, "No matter what the weather looks like, we have to go ahead now. Waiting any longer could be even more dangerous. So let's move it." As a result of this decision, D-Day was the beginning of the end of World War II. Eisenhower's decision behind the decision was to stop thinking about it and take action. If you're waiting for the best time to act, you may wait forever.

"There is a point at which we have to make a leap of faith, the point after which the right decision becomes wrong because it has been made too late."
— JOE GRIFFITH

Author Lauri Beth Jones, in her book *Jesus, CEO*, describes a classic example of what it takes to "jump." She writes:

"A year ago my mother went to visit an art gallery in Sedona, Arizona. After Mom oohed and aahed about how lucky the woman working there was to live in such a hauntingly beautiful part of the country, the woman said, "Why don't you move here?" Mom immediately replied that she didn't think she could afford to live there. The woman laughed and said, "You think I'm made of money? No way. But one day I decided that this is where I wanted to live, so I up and moved here. You can too." Then she gave her a list of real estate offices to visit. On the way home Mom kept saying to herself, "That woman lives in Sedona. Why not me?" She went home to El Paso, praying the whole way, put her home of thirty-four years on the market, sold it that day to a man who had always admired it, and within sixty days she was sipping tea on her new balcony in Sedona."

This story illustrates the power of plunging through your fears. When you stop wallowing in anxiety and excuses for not doing what you really want to do and take that irreversible first step, like selling your house or quitting your job, momentum carries you the rest of the way. Now there is no going back.

Once Lauri Beth Jones' mom sold her house, she was committed. She had to move. Why not live in the place of her dreams? Once the decision was made, she set in motion the forces that would carry her the rest of the way. Sixty short days later, she was in her new house in Sedona — the result of massive energy focused on a single objective. Once you decide what you really want to do and commit all of your energy and resources to it, nothing can stop you.

> "*Until one is committed there is hesitancy, the chance to draw back, always ineffectiveness. Concerning all acts of initiative (and creation), there is one elementary truth, the ignorance of which kills countless ideas and splendid plans: that the moment one definitely commits oneself, then Providence moves too. All sorts of things occur to help one that could never otherwise have occurred. A whole stream of events issues from the decision, raising in one's favour all manner of unforeseen incidents and meetings and material assistance, which no man could have dreamt would have come his way.*"
> — W.H. MURRAY

A classic example from antiquity of jumping through your fears occurred on January 10, 49 B.C. On that day, Julius Caesar was forced to make a critical choice. The Roman Senate, fearing Caesar's increasing military power, ordered him to give up his command. In previous years,

Caesar had formed the First Triumvirate, in which he, Pompey, and Marcus Licinius Crassus formed a powerful alliance. However, over time, Pompey became concerned with Caesar's increasing military might and was now aligned with the Roman Senate. Standing on the banks of the Rubicon River with his 5,000 troops behind him, Caesar had to make a decision. On the other side of the river were Pompey's troops in the province of Cisalpine Gaul (the Po Valley). Caesar and other Roman governors were forbidden to cross this boundary with troops. Crossing the boundary would have been considered an act of hostility and would have started a civil war. Yet, Caesar's only other option was to surrender his command. Caesar crossed the Rubicon and engaged Pompey's troops, who surrendered almost immediately. Pompey was forced to flee to the Balkans. Sixty days later, Caesar became the master of the Roman world. That same year, Caesar declared himself dictator and consul.

Today, the phrase "crossing the Rubicon" is often used to describe a decision from which there is no turning back. When Caesar crossed the Rubicon with his troops, this act alone began a civil war from which there was no turning back. Caesar's momentum carried him the rest of his way. Had Caesar not made the decision to cross the Rubicon, he never would have achieved his great victory.

Another compelling example is the story of the firemen of the New York Fire Department who ran headlong into the burning World Trade Center when everyone else was running out on that fateful day of September 11, 2001. What was it within these men that compelled them to sacrifice their lives, not knowing for certain that they would even be able to save anyone? What was it in the fiber of their very souls that made them literally jump through the fire that day? They saw something different from what the people fleeing the fire saw. Oh, of course, they saw the fire. But the firemen also saw the purpose on the other side of the fire and that's what they chose to focus on. That's what heroes do.

Our heroes have often been superstar athletes, movie stars, senators, presidents, and TV personalities. But many of them left us disappointed, disillusioned, and embarrassed. More and more, our heroes are the average everyday people who go out of their way to help someone else.

True heroes see a purpose bigger than themselves, their money, or their fame. Todd Beamer, Tom Burnett Jr., and Jeremy Glick are just such heroes. On September 11, 2001, terrorists had already crashed airplanes into both towers of the World Trade Center. Beamer, Burnett, and Glick were on United Airlines Fight 93, which was still in the air and had been taken over by terrorists. They knew they were going to die. But they decided to try to save others' lives in the process. Unarmed, untrained, and unprepared, they decided to take back the plane.

Before they moved out, Burnett spoke to his wife by cell phone. "We're all going to die but there are three of us who are going to do something about it." Jeremy Glick also spoke to his wife. Initially she begged him to sit down and not call attention to himself. She begged him to do whatever he could to save himself. But he explained that it was not that sort of situation. *There was much more at stake than personal survival.* Beamer said a prayer with the GTE operator and together they quoted the Lord's Prayer and the 23rd Psalm. The operator stayed on the line and heard Beamer say, "Are you guys ready? Let's roll." His wife, Lisa Beamer, says that this was the expression Todd used every time they were getting ready to leave the house on a family outing. The cockpit voice recorder captured sounds of people shouting and screaming in the cabin and cockpit shortly before the crash. But together, Glick, Burnett, and Beamer succeeded. In the fight that ensued, the plane crashed into a field somewhere south of Pittsburgh, Pennsylvania, instead of its intended target in Washington, D.C.

When the United States retaliated by invading Afghanistan, an outstanding professional football player for the Arizona Cardinals answered the call to arms. Pat Tillman traded a $3.6 million, three-year contract with the Cardinals for an Army Ranger job that paid $18,000 per year. Earlier that year he had turned down a $9 million, five-year contract with Super Bowl champions, the St. Louis Rams. He turned it down out of loyalty to the Cardinals. In a society where superstar athletes whine that a $20 million deal just isn't enough, his actions are baffling.

And then, why did Tillman enlist in the army? Playing in the NFL is every high school football player's dream come true. You become an instant millionaire. You become instantly famous and instantly secure. Why would anyone in their right mind give this up? We just don't get it. It doesn't compute. Heroes see a purpose bigger than themselves.

Tillman was first sent to Iraq with the 75th Regiment Ranger Battalion during Operation Iraqi Freedom. Then he was transferred to Afghanistan where U.S. troops had been battling pockets of al Qaeda and Taliban resistance. Despite major efforts by the media to make him a hero when he gave up the NFL to fight the terrorists, Tillman refused to let himself be treated any differently from his fellow soldiers. He refused to talk to the press — except for one rare interview. In that interview he said, "My family has ... gone and fought in wars and I really haven't done a damn thing as far as laying myself on the line like that, and so I have a great deal of respect for those that have and what the flag stands for." Tillman was later killed by friendly fire in Afghanistan.

Dave McGinnis, former head coach of the Cardinals said, "Pat Tillman made a decision based on some very real values, and the words honor, dignity, integrity, commitment... they were not just adjectives with Pat Tillman, they were reality in his life, and that came through very loud and clear." Heroes don't look for what's in it for them. They see the bigger purpose.

But heroes come in all shapes and sizes. In September 2004, in the little town of Beslan in Russia, a group of masked men stormed a middle school and took the whole school hostage. A young 17-year-old girl named Karina Begayeva had a chance to escape with other children who had hidden in the boiler room. But she turned back and ran into the school gymnasium where most of the other kids were being held. Why would she do this? She saw what others could not see. Her brother was in there. She knew that her brother could not walk because of his withered leg. Over the next three days, the terrorists made all of the children strip down to their underwear and refused to give them food or water. When the children cried, they shot rifles into the air and threatened to kill them if they did not stop crying. They forced them to drink their own urine. After three days without food or water, the children began to grow weak and sick.

Outside the building, 10,000 Russian troops kept watch, waiting for an opportunity to negotiate a peaceful solution or to strike. Suddenly, the sounds of an explosion and gunfire filled the air. Naked schoolchildren ran from the school, being shot at by the terrorists as they fled. Russian special forces stormed the building. Relatives screamed in helpless horror.

When the first bomb blast erupted, a piece of shrapnel tore through Karina's left foot. Half blinded by the blast and choking on the dense smoke, she could barely stand. But she knew she only had a few seconds to get herself and her brother to safety. She somehow managed to reach for her brother's arm and half-carry, half-drag him along in the midst of the chaos as a firefight between the terrorists and the Russian special forces erupted all around them. She managed to scramble out through a broken window, where Russian police ran up and whisked them away. Karina Begayeva is what heroes are made of.

When you know what needs to be done, you must make an internal decision to stop thinking about it, stop overanalyzing, and just do it. This is the decision behind the decision — to focus on a purpose bigger than yourself.

When you focus on a purpose that is bigger than yourself, you see things that others cannot see. When you believe in a cause that is worth fighting for, you can do almost anything. Age, size, gender, skills, and equipment do not matter. If you have a big enough reason *why*, you can always find the answer to *how*.

THE DECISION BEHIND THE DECISION:
Heroes CHOOSE to focus on
a purpose bigger than themselves.

HEROES CAN SEE INTO THE FUTURE

"When you encounter difficulties and contradictions do not try to break them, but bend them with gentleness and time."
— ST. FRANCIS DE SALES

When you learn to see through the eyes of heroes, be careful because you might see a cause or a purpose that is much bigger than yourself. The things you see might cause you to dream, and the things you dream may be things that cannot be achieved in your lifetime. And those dreams might get you into a world of trouble.

Martin Luther King, Jr. never saw his dreams fulfilled in his lifetime. Yet, before he died he said to us all, "I say to you today, my friends, that in spite of the difficulties and frustrations of the moment, I still have a dream." Neither he nor Rosa Parks, who almost single-handedly started the civil rights movement in the 1960's, were satisfied with their experience in the present. They both realized that things had to become worse before they got better. The status quo was no longer acceptable and they had to stir things up. They were willing to stir up the hornet's nest in the short term, even though it meant they would be stung, in order to improve the lot of blacks in the long term.

Some problems have been brewing for a long time. They did not just crop up overnight. There are no quick fixes for these types of problems. They can only be fixed through consistent, long-term effort. Solid granite boulders can be reduced to sand, but only through the rocking of ocean waves, the rushing of rivers, the whispering of the wind, and the gentleness of time.

Martin Luther King, Jr. recognized that we can't have everything we want overnight. There is no rushing the harvest. You can make instant Cream of Wheat, but there is no such thing as instant wheat crops. In order to create wheat crops, the earth must be tilled, the seed must be planted, the soil must be fertilized, the seed must be watered, it must germinate, and it must receive plenty of sunlight. The sun must rise and set. The farmer must wait patiently. There is no rushing this process. This is the only way to see and enjoy the fruits of your labor. Hard work now pays off later — after a sufficient amount of time has passed. There is no way around daily hard work applied consistently over a long period of time.

> *"How poor are they that have not patience!*
> *What wound did ever heal but by degree."*
> — WILLIAM SHAKESPEARE

Some things are worth waiting for. Successful careers don't happen overnight. A quality college education, a master's degree, and a Ph.D. all take years to obtain. Artists, musicians, and authors know it takes years to develop a reputation and a following. For every success we achieve, we usually experience a multitude of failures along the way. Each failure has the potential to teach us something. Each failure brings us a little closer to our goal. It wasn't until Lee Iacocca was fired from Ford in 1978 that he went to Chrysler and became famous for turning the company around. Time, patience, and hard work yielded the victory and the fame. The tragedy of being fired from Ford merely opened the door to greater opportunities elsewhere. Remember, the significance of any "tragedy" cannot be determined until enough time has passed.

> *"In the middle of difficulty, lies opportunity."*
> — ALBERT EINSTEIN

The term "starving artist" comes from the fact that many artists live on next to nothing in order to pursue their art careers full-time. They are betting that the hard work and sacrifices they make in the short term will pay off in the long term. The same applies to struggling actors, musicians, and authors. Those who endure will be victorious. The victory is not always great riches. But remember, the real victory is simply being able to spend your life pursuing what makes you happy.

> *"Do not be desirous of having things done quickly. Do not look at small advantages. Desire to have things done quickly prevents their being done thoroughly. Looking at small advantages prevents great affairs from being accomplished."*
> — CONFUCIUS

Many people say, "Live for today, for tomorrow may never come" ... *"Carpe diem"* (Seize the day!) ... "Eat, drink, and be merry, for tomorrow we may die," or "Live each day like it was your last." Marilyn Monroe once said, "Ever notice how 'what the hell' is always the right decision?"

Although these philosophies are inspiring and can motivate us toward great accomplishments, they can also cause us to act rashly without considering the long-term consequences. Clearly, there must be a balance. If you spend all of your time, energy, and money seeking immediate pleasure and satisfaction, then what will you have to show for it in the long run? On the other hand, if you defer all pleasure to another day and live only for tomorrow, you'll miss some of life's greatest pleasures that are available to you now.

I know of several men who worked their whole lives and saved all their money so that they could retire and finally do the things they loved, only to die within a few months after they retired. What a tragedy. One of them was a friend of mine. I have made up my mind not to be like them. Yes, I know how to work hard, but I am squeezing every ounce of adventure out of life along the way. Jumping out of airplanes. Scuba diving with sea turtles in Maui. Playing with lion cubs in Africa. Most of America's millionaires and billionaires didn't get that way by saving money over the long haul. They became wealthy by being daring and taking the risks others were not willing to take.

There is something to be learned from the men who saved all their money and then died just shortly after they retired. You shouldn't defer your greatest dreams and the things you love to do for another day. Some of life's most satisfying moments come from spontaneous, totally outrageous, "throw caution to the wind" kind of fun. Sometimes, like Marilyn Monroe, you just have to say "what the hell" and go for it. For the most part, this kind of enjoyment is extremely satisfying, but it isn't long-lasting and it may have long-term consequences. Enjoy it for what it is, but only after you've considered the long-term consequences *or benefits.*

Scientific studies have proven that those who have the discipline to delay gratification score higher on SAT tests, get into better colleges, and are generally more successful in life. In 1970, Walter Mischel conducted an experiment on four year olds in a room with a bell and a marshmallow. If the kids rang the bell, Mischel would come into the room and give them *one* marshmallow. If they did not ring the bell and waited for Mischel to come into the room on his own, he would give them *two* marshmallows. Some kids broke down and rang the bell in just a few minutes. Others lasted fifteen minutes. The kids were studied over the rest of their lives. Those who waited the longest did better on SAT exams, got into better colleges, and generally had higher incomes. Those who rang the bell the quickest tended to become bullies, and received worse teacher evaluations and were more likely to have drug problems. This test confirms what we already inherently know. Greater rewards await those who have the discipline and patience to persevere.

But seeing into the future isn't always about "what's in it for me?" The Native Americans have a beautiful philosophy about preserving the earth for future generations that is expressed profoundly in the following statement:

> *"In our way of life, in our government, with every decision we make, we always keep in mind the Seventh Generation to come. It's our job to see that the people coming ahead, the generations still unborn, have a world no worse than ours — and hopefully better. When we walk upon Mother Earth we always*

plant our feet carefully because we know the faces of our future generations are looking up at us from beneath the ground. We never forget them."

— OREN LYONS, "ONANDAGA FAITHKEEPER"

Thousands of years ago, the Native Americans could see things the newly arrived Europeans could not see. They could see into the future. Was this a spiritual gift? No. They *chose* to see the future and this was their genius.

The Native Americans are not the only ones who could see into the future. This genius was also beautifully expressed by the great composer Ludwig van Beethoven. One day, after listening to Beethoven's *String Quartet in F*, one of his critics, composer Muzio Clementi, said to him, "Surely you don't consider these works to be music." To which Beethoven replied, "Oh, they are not for you. They are for a later age." That age was *today* and Beethoven had the vision to foresee it. Today, everyone has heard of Beethoven. Who, besides my good friend Dan Stephens, has ever heard of Clementi?

Human beings are slowly learning how important it is to put future interests on an equal footing with the present interests. Some third world countries are finally realizing that they can make more money and protect their people's financial future by protecting their natural resources rather than by selling them off. On August 1, 2002, President El Jadj Omar Bongo, the leader of a small West African country, Gabon, created 13 national parks, protecting one of the world's last true jungle paradises (11,000 square miles) from loggers. In the Ivindo National Park, there is a paradise within a paradise called Langoue Bai (only recently named), where elephants, gorillas, monkeys, crocodiles, large forest antelopes, parrots, and all manner of birds come to greet each other and play in a river fed by waterfalls. When these areas were first explored in 2000 by J. Michael Faye, most of these animals had never before seen human contact. It was and is a true Eden. Now it is protected, and the future of the country will be enhanced and preserved by eco-tourism.

President Bongo helped his country and the world see that we are better off preserving our natural resources than exploiting them in the present for short-term gain.

Some causes are bigger than life. They are bigger than me and you and all of our problems put together. Some causes cannot be achieved in our lifetime. If we open our eyes, we will see them. But once we see them, we will have a decision to make.

THE DECISION BEHIND THE DECISION:
Heroes can see into the future because they CHOOSE to see into the future.

HEROES HARVEST THEIR HIDDEN GIFTS

*"I always wanted to be somebody,
but I should have been more specific."*
— LILY TOMLIN

Best-selling author Zig Ziglar tells a story about a man at the turn of the century who owned a piece of land. Due to a severe drought, the man was forced to start selling off his land bit by bit to feed his family. It was a crisis situation. One day an oil company representative came to him and asked for permission to explore for oil on his property. The man had nothing to lose and everything to gain. He agreed. When they struck oil, the gush of oil caused a huge explosion that obliterated the wooden derrick. The well flowed for many days before it could be capped; over 100,000 barrels per day flowed out. In the first year, the well produced more than 15 million barrels of oil. The well became known around the world as Spindletop.

People said he had become a millionaire overnight, but this was not true. He was a millionaire all along. He just didn't see it. Once he saw what he had, he chose to do everything within his power to harvest it. But harvesting is hard work. First, someone had to explore the land and discover the treasure that lay dormant. Second, they had to harvest it by bringing it to the surface and putting it into barrels. Third, they had to take it to market it in order to get the most value for it. Fourth, they had to negotiate the price and close the deal. Only then would the hidden treasure be of any value to anyone.

How does this story relate to your life? Sometimes a crisis forces us to look for resources and gifts we never knew we had. But opening your eyes and looking for your gifts is a conscious choice. It requires deliberate action — and it is only the first step. Then you have to work hard to develop those gifts and make them of use to someone.

Have you ever thought there might be something beautiful and powerful deep inside of you, like the oil in the story, yearning to be released? People have a natural desire to realize their full potential. We all long to be needed for our unique skills and talents. We all desire that our hidden potential be "discovered," just as an oil driller discovers oil beneath the surface. Our desire to feel significant in this life keeps us moving forward. It is a craving that must be satisfied. Something inside tells us it is not enough just to collect a paycheck or simply meet basic living expenses day in and day out.

"Life is either a daring adventure or nothing."
— HELEN KELLER

Life's pressures have a way of squeezing needs that lie deep within us to the surface. These can be needs that we may have been ignoring for years, or things about ourselves that we may have been unwilling to acknowledge. Events in our lives have a way of sending us messages about the direction we should go. Don't ignore these messages.

"Stir up the gift that is within you."
— ST. PAUL'S LETTER TO TIMOTHY

I once had a dream in which I saw a dark, black volcano. Out of the volcano poured a river of molten gold, flowing in all directions, like a pot of boiling water when it overflows. Flowing on the river were millions of glittering diamonds of all sizes and colors that came tumbling out of the mountain when it erupted. This dream was so real, the colors were so startling, that it woke me up. I was left wondering why I'd had this dream. While I pondered the dream somewhere in that foggy world between sleep and awake, I heard a soft small voice say, "You have many gifts to give."

I realized that all the talent in the world, if left inside, can never be enjoyed. If we leave our gifts inside ourselves, no one will ever see or benefit from them. What is the use of having these gifts if you do not use them to make the world a better place? What is the use of having these gifts if you never use them to make someone happy? What is the good of hoarding what you have? You've got to give these gifts away in order to enjoy them. You've got to give yourself away.

"A musician must make music,
an artist must paint,
a poet must write,
if he is to be ultimately at peace with himself."
— ABRAHAM MASLOW

If you are currently in a job you hate and it requires all of your energy just to force yourself to get up and go to work, life is trying to tell you something. If you find it exhausting just to complete a simple task, not because it's hard but because you find it uninteresting, you should view this as a road sign. You may be on the wrong course.

The first step toward knowing what you want out of life is being true to yourself. This is the decision behind the decision. This requires that you learn to listen to what your inner voice is saying. If you follow a course because it's the most consistent with who you are, you are more likely to succeed than if you follow a course that is not consistent with who you are. If you're doing something you hate, you are more likely to keep doing a poor job of it so that at some point you don't have to do it any longer. It only makes sense to follow your strengths. Most people wish they had the guts to try. Whatever you do, do it with all your heart. This is the only way to truly succeed in life and become a whole person.

Follow your natural interests and desires. Do what you are naturally good at. If you don't know what you are naturally good at, do what makes you feel good inside and satisfied with life. Do what makes you feel whole and complete. You are more likely to succeed at something you enjoy than something you don't enjoy.

> *"Whatever it is that you do, when you really want something it's because that desire originated in the soul of the universe. It's your mission on earth."*
>
> — Paulo Coelho

I am convinced that our instincts and desires do not happen by accident. They act as internal steering mechanisms to guide us. What have people always said you are good at or would be good at if you pursued it? What do you have a burning desire to do? What is your inner voice telling you about the direction you should go? What goals and dreams have you delayed pursuing? Stop ignoring your inner promptings and longings.

When was the last time you made a list of things that truly give you satisfaction in life? How often and with what amount of intensity are you currently pursuing these things? Are you currently enduring a less than satisfactory situation when you know in your heart you should be doing something else? Are you making excuses for not pursuing your dreams? If you held your excuses in one hand and your dreams in the other, which hand would have more weight? If you think following your dream is a luxury you don't deserve and you don't have the time or money to pursue it, then you have made a decision that will carve out your place in history — anonymity. But it's never too late to change your mind. It's only too late on the day you choose to give up. This could happen when you are 65 or it could happen when you are 25. Giving up is a choice you make, not something that happens to you.

> *"We will either find a way or make one."*
> — HANNIBAL

Be willing to experiment with something new. There are new adventures around every corner.

You may be on the cutting edge of a new trend or discovery that will change conventional wisdom for years to come. You may not go down in history, but you may change the course of your life and the lives of those around you for the better. Only time will tell.

It's never too late to decide what you want to be when you grow up. We should be on a never-ending quest to achieve our best and highest purpose, no matter what stage of life we find ourselves in. Remember, the decisions you make today affect your future more than the decisions you made yesterday.

Life is a little bit like fly fishing. When I first learned to fly fish, it was awkward because there was no weight on the end of the line to aid in casting. The casting is all done with a rhythmic motion of the arm and shoulder and a flick of the wrist. It requires a great deal of finesse. On the day of my first lesson, it was very windy. I thought attempting to cast an almost weightless fly line into the wind was a pointless exercise. But my instructor did it with great ease. He told me that in fly fishing you have to pick a spot on the water where you want your fly to land and cast toward it. If you don't pick a particular spot and keep directing your energies toward it, your fly line will be tossed about by the wind. The same is true in life. You need to pick a specific goal and keep casting toward it. Otherwise, random winds will blow you someplace you didn't choose.

In order to get to your goal, you need to make two decisions. First, decide where to cast your hook. Second, make a decision every day to do something that is specifically designed to pull you closer to the goal. Ask yourself, "What specific action can I take today to get me a little closer to my goal?" If you don't know where to start, begin by reading articles and books about what you want to do. Talk to people who are already successfully doing it. But don't just sit there. Act!

Setting specific goals is very powerful. Writing down your "big picture" desires of where you want to be in ten years is critical. Today, you should stop and create a "dream sheet" of where you want to be and what you want to be doing in ten years. For now, ignore whether these dreams sound realistic or not. The key is to let your imagination run wild. Start dreaming now. Leave out no option. Deprive yourself of nothing. Make your list today!

Why is this exercise so important? Goal-setting creates the framework around which all other decisions can be made. Your goals become the standard upon which all options are evaluated. If a certain choice does not bring you closer to your goal, it should not be seriously considered. This simplifies what might have been a difficult decision. In short, we should reject all options that take us off the course that leads us to our goals. If you don't make a specific choice about where you want to be, then you can't make the daily decisions designed to get you there.

When you chart a new course on paper by writing down your goals, you give your mind a new pattern to follow. This is part of restructuring the "programs" in your mind. You can't pursue a new direction until you allow yourself to do so in your mind. You've got to free yourself mentally to follow a new course. When you write down specific dreams and tangible goals, you give your mind guideposts to follow. You give your mind little handholds to reach for and hold onto one by one as you climb the mountain. When your mind starts following a new pattern, your actions follow. When your actions change, the results you get out of life also change.

> *"Sow a thought, and you reap an action;*
> *sow an action, and you reap a habit;*
> *sow a habit, and you reap a character;*
> *sow a character, and you reap a destiny."*
> — CHARLES READE

Writing down your thoughts is important because it transforms what is vague and general in your mind into specific bite-sized and achievable tasks. But you've got to be specific about what you write. Writing down on paper what is floating around in your mind is like trapping exotic butterflies and examining them up close in order to identify them. While they are flitting about, we only get passing glimpses of their beautiful colors and wing patterns. We sense that they are there, but we don't know exactly what they are, where they came from, or where they are going. They are more like a fantasy than a reality. When we capture these specific thoughts with pen and paper, we can examine them more clearly. You give your mind something concrete and tangible to *focus* on. Remember, what you focus on determines what you *believe*. If you are not focusing on something narrow and specific, then your beliefs will be vague and nebulous.

When you create a very specific picture in your head of who you want to be and what you want to accomplish, and focus on it every day, the mind does an amazing thing. It turns this image into a blueprint of what you will become. A perfect example comes from the life of well-known comedian George Lopez.

When he was only a child, Lopez was abandoned first by his father and later by his mother. He was raised by an abusive grandmother and an alcoholic grandfather. On top of that, he was raised in poverty. To escape his misery, he *chose* to focus on comedy. His favorite comedian was Freddie Prinze. Every day after school he watched episodes of *Chico and the Man*. He hung a picture of Freddie Prinze on his bedroom wall and stared at it every night.

What he focused on began to shape what he believed. This was the Second Law of Critical Focus™ at work. He began to say to himself, "I can be a comic. I can do what Freddie is doing. I want to make people laugh." When he was still a teenager, he wrote these words on a scratch piece of paper: "I know at times I can't make it but eventually I will. And I will hit the American people like a hammer. I will be the best." These were powerful words because he spoke as if what he was saying was fact. He didn't say "I hope to" or "I would like to." If you look carefully at what he wrote, you will see that he used phrases such as, "I *know* . . ." He said, "I *will* . . ." "I *will*. . ." "I *will* . . ."

What he didn't realize was that he was imprinting in his brain an exact image of what he *would* become, and he was burning it in deep — with *words* and *pictures.*

This imprint was burned so deeply into his mind that even though he bombed at club after club, and even after he had abandoned his dream for years and come back and quit again, *the imprint was still there.* It would ultimately determine who he would become — against all odds.

Eventually George Lopez went on to become one of the best known comedians in all of America. He has performed for the President of the United States and other celebrities. He went on to have his own prime time comedy show, which was named after him, *The George Lopez Show.* He even wrote a book about his life called *Why You Crying?*

This was not a miracle. It was not the product of fate or divine intervention. It was the result of all of the principles heroes have followed for thousands of years. What you *focus* on determines what you believe. What you *believe* determines what you expect out of life. What you *expect* determines what you see. What you see determines the options that are available to you. Lopez set his destiny in motion when he *chose* to focus, over and over, day in and day out, on a specific, tangible, and literal image (a photo) of who he wanted to become. Then he set that focus in concrete by using powerful words to seal it in.

You too have the freedom to choose what to focus on no matter what is going on in the world around you. This is the Seventh Law of Critical Focus™. You too can *choose* to use the power of your imagination to focus on a specific, tangible image of who you want to become. You have the power to *choose* the words and pictures you need to help you keep that focus.

The more narrow and specific the picture, the easier it is to create an imprint in your brain. The more specific the imprint in your brain, the more likely it is your life will conform to that image.

> *"There is a law in psychology that if you form a picture in your mind of what you would like to be, and you keep and hold that picture there long enough, you will soon become exactly as you have been thinking."*
> — WILLIAM JAMES

In order to help narrow your focus, sit down and itemize the specifics of what you are seeking. Create a picture of it in your head. Find a picture of it and tape it to your bathroom mirror. Make a list of the details, the colors, the people, and the money it will take to get there. What do you see yourself doing in ten years? More importantly, *who* do you see yourself *being*? Who are the people that surround you? What kind of car do you drive? What kind of house do you live in?

Where is it? What color is it? Is it stone or brick or wood? How big is it? What do you see when you step outside your front door? Dream it. Love it. Live it. Act as if it's real and it will become real.

> *"What if you slept?*
> *And what if, in your sleep, you dreamed?*
> *And what if, in your dream,*
> *you went to heaven and there plucked a*
> *strange and beautiful flower?*
> *And what if, when you awoke, you had the*
> *flower in your hand?"*
>
> — SAMUEL TAYLOR COLERIDGE

Once you have a clear and specific vision in mind, try plotting the steps working backward from there to where you are now. This is called beginning with the end in mind. If you know where you want to end up, you can plan on how to get there.

Someone once explained it this way: Every ship captain knows his next port of call. He knows where it is, and he knows how to get there, even though he cannot see it for 99% of his voyage. He launches out knowing where he is going. But every day he focuses all of his energies on the little tasks designed to get him there. He keeps repeating this proven pattern of behavior daily until he gets there, making any needed adjustments along the way.

A life without goals is like a ship without a rudder. A ship without a rudder gets blown and tossed about by every wind and every current that comes along. Is your life constantly being tossed about by things over which you feel you have no control? By the latest fad or money-making idea? You can avoid this by giving yourself some specific and attainable goals from which you make a definite commitment not to waver.

An excellent example of this comes from the survival story of mountaineer Joe Simpson in his book *Touching The Void*. In 1985, Simpson broke his leg on his descent of a 20,000-foot mountain in the Peruvian Andes. Then after a second fall left him dangling in midair off a cliff, his partner, Simon Yates, had no choice but to cut the rope that tied them together. Failure to cut the rope meant that gravity would eventually pull them both off the steep mountain face to their deaths.

The rope snapped with the touch of Yates' blade and Simpson dropped into a long, narrow, vertical ice tube with no way to get to the top. His body came to rest precariously on a narrow ice bridge between two gaping vertical drops. He had two choices. He could either sit there until death slowly overtook his freezing body, or he could plunge into the dark unknown to meet death on his own terms. He had one ice screw left, which he banged into the wall of ice. Then he threaded his rope through it and somehow managed to tie a crude knot in the end of it. This would be his anchor as he lowered his body into the deep, dark, icy unknown. He could not see the bottom of the ice tube — he could see only a cold, cruel, black hole. He had no idea if the end of the rope even touched the bottom. He purposely did not tie a knot in the end of the rope, which would have stopped his descent, preferring instead to plunge to his death rather than dangle in midair and slowly freeze to death.

To his surprise, his body eventually came to rest on a flat surface of snow. But it turned out to be only an eggshell-thin layer of snow that was keeping gravity from sucking his body into the blackness. Then he saw a thin ray of light shining from the opposite side of the cavern. There was a 45-degree slope of ice leading up to where he could see a pinpoint of daylight. This was the way out — if only he could reach it.

He lay flat and shimmied gently across the thin layer of snow until he reached the other side of the cavern. But with a badly broken leg, the slope of ice looked impossible to climb.

He came up with a plan. He would bend over and dig a small foothold for each of his boots, which were equipped with crampons (metal claws) for climbing. Then he would pound his ice axes in the wall of ice above him and slowly lift his bad leg, then his good leg into the footholds, while pulling his body up with the ice axes. Each time he put weight on his bad leg, searing pain exploded up and down his leg. He would scream and curse out loud — his own words mocking him as they echoed through the hollow, frozen tube. Then he would repeat the process.

He made a decision to focus on the pattern rather than the pain. "The flares of pain became merged into the routine and I paid less attention to them, concentrating solely on the patterns." He was so intent on focusing on the pattern that he refused to even look up to the object of his climb for fear that it would remind him of the little progress he had made and how far he still had to go. He knew where he was going, but it was more important to focus on the pattern. The pattern was working — one inch at a time, but it was working. After what seemed like an eternity, he popped his head up through the snow to see a ring of spectacularly beautiful mountains and blue sky. He had made it. But now he had to figure out a way to get down the rest of the mountain with a broken leg.

Simpson would be forced to repeat different patterns of behavior, standing, then falling forward, then crawling, then standing and falling forward again, for several days and nights without food or water. He would pick a spot in the distance and focus on it. Then he would give himself a deadline by which he had to get to it. When he finally got there, he would pick out another spot in the distance and repeat the pattern. Depending on the terrain, he would figure out a different pattern of movement that was most likely to push his body forward. Once he found the right pattern, he would simply focus on the pattern and repeat it over and over until he got to the next spot. It was a slow, agonizing process and his body got weaker and weaker as he went. Through the sheer force of his will and the voice inside his head that kept commanding his mangled body forward like a cruel drill sergeant, after several days, he finally got close enough to his campsite where his shouts could be heard. When his climbing partner found him, Simpson didn't even look like himself. His face was bloody and scarred from falling repeatedly and from frostbite. His arms and legs were shredded from the rocks and ice. His leg had swollen to almost the size of his waist. But he was alive.

What saved Joe Simpson was his decision to focus on a short, achievable goal and give himself a deadline to reach it. It was when he stopped pushing himself to get there by the deadline that he started to lose hope. He explains that his destination had become "a vague aim instead of a carefully planned objective. Without timing each stage, I had drifted aimlessly with no sense of urgency. Today it had to be different."

Simpson had one other thing going for him. For part of his journey, he could see the blurred footprints of his climbing partner, showing him the best path down the mountain. He followed the trail until the wind and a new dusting of snow made the tracks disappear.

What can we learn from Joe Simpson's epic tale of survival?

- First, in order to survive and prosper in times of adversity, you have to know what your final destination is and keep it always in your mind.

- Second, break up the journey into small, achievable stages.

- Third, experiment until you find a pattern of behavior that pulls you inch by inch closer to your goal.

- Fourth, count on failing over and over while trying to find the right pattern. Then count on falling again even after you have found the right pattern. But make a decision to fall forward — in the direction of your goal.

- Fifth, if the goal seems impossible, focus on the pattern rather than the pain.

- Sixth, realize that the pattern of behavior that got you to your first small goal may not work for the second-stage goal. Each goal has its own unique challenges, risks, and rewards. Each stage will have its own unique kind of pain. Find the pattern of behavior that works for each stage of the journey.

■ Seventh, if you can see the footprints of someone who knows the way and has been there before, follow them. Eventually you will arrive at your final destination. You might be bloody, beat up, and in pain, but you will get there. The key is — find the pattern that works and repeat it.

Once you have decided what your goals are, the decision behind the decision is that every day you will repeat a pattern of behavior that you know is slowly pulling you closer and closer to your goal. This is how ordinary people become heroes.

THE DECISION BEHIND THE DECISION:
Heroes CHOOSE to focus on a small, specific picture
of where they want to be and repeat a successful
pattern of behavior daily until they get there.

HEROES FOCUS ON INTANGIBLE VALUES

> *"Many persons have a wrong idea of
> what constitutes true happiness. It is not
> attained through self-gratification,
> but through fidelity to a worthy purpose."*
>
> — HELEN KELLER

Sometimes the only way to overcome a tangible problem is with an intangible solution. But it takes special vision to see the intangible solution. When Billy Joel was a young man, he loved music. But it can be difficult to make a living as a musician. When he was young, he spent many nights singing in dimly lit bars, playing the piano for drunks and people who were too busy talking to notice he was there. He was a high school dropout with no experience. Getting a regular paying job was pretty tough. He was so poor he slept in laundromats. But he kept working, kept trying, and kept pursuing his passion with all of his heart. He made some tough decisions along the way. He decided never to sell out his soul for financial security. He decided never to give up. By following his passion, he ultimately found not only financial security but also great wealth and fame. The rewards speak for themselves. Billy Joel put intangible values above tangible financial needs and he was rewarded in the end.

"For what shall it profit a man if
he gains the whole world and loses his own soul?"
— MATTHEW 16:26

Most of the world's religions and the most respected leaders of all time teach that we must have a central focus to our lives and a purpose around which all other things revolve. When we have this, everything else falls into place. Stephen Covey, in his book *The Seven Habits of Highly Effective People*, explains that in order to be truly successful, we must focus on the intangibles of life — on those things that give life meaning.

Kahlil Gibran said, "All work is empty save when there is love, for work is love made visible."

The Sioux Indians teach that when you focus on spiritual things and keep your mind centered on a specific intangible purpose instead of fretting over the daily business of living, everything else falls into place.

Henry David Thoreau said, "There is no more fatal blunder than he who consumes the greater part of his life getting his living."

Jesus Christ said, "Seek ye first the kingdom of God and all these things shall be added unto you."

Albert Schweitzer said, "I don't know what your destiny will be, but one thing I know: The only ones among you who will be truly happy are those who have sought and found how to serve."

Viktor Frankl said, "Success . . . is the unintended side effect of one's personal dedication to a cause greater than oneself or as the byproduct of one's surrender to a person other than oneself."

Winston Churchill said, "We make a living by what we get, but we make a life by what we give."

Even Lance Armstrong said, "An athlete has to somehow figure out how to enrich the people around himself. Otherwise, he's purposeless."

The Jews, the Hindus, the Buddhists, the Christians, and even the agnostics all agree — when your life revolves around a central purpose, life's practical issues have a way of working themselves out and satisfaction with life is the net result.

If you're not putting your time and energies into the things that bring satisfaction to your soul and give life meaning for you, then you aren't fulfilling your best and highest purpose. You're spinning your wheels and biding your time until retirement while your soul withers on the vine. When you give up your dreams, you die a little bit inside with each passing day.

"The mass of men lead lives of quiet desperation."
— HENRY DAVID THOREAU

If you aren't doing what you are doing with a passion, then why are you doing it at all? When you find something you can really do with a passion, it's worthwhile to make the sacrifices and take the risks necessary in order to pursue it. There is a parable about a man who searched all his life for a pearl of great value. When he finally found it, he sold all he had in order to buy it. When you find something you can do with passion, something that gives your life meaning, you should be ready and willing to do whatever it takes to pursue it. Better to be poor and happy than financially secure and miserable.

But how do you balance these lofty intangible goals with the hardcore financial necessities of the day? When you can't afford to put gas in your car or pay the light bill or the rent, somehow finding a well-paying job seems to take precedence over pursuing lofty dreams. But this doesn't have to be the case. It is all a matter of your priorities. Remember, everything you do in life is a matter of choice.

Going back to the Billy Joel story, you might be tempted to say, "Yes, but I am no Billy Joel. Billy Joel is loaded with talent. He was destined to succeed. I could never be like that." I respectfully disagree. I doubt that when Billy Joel was sleeping in laundromats he was thinking, "Wait a minute. I'm Billy Joel. I'm destined to succeed." And yet, while he was sleeping on the laundromat floor, he possessed everything he needed to succeed.

History is filled with examples of now-famous people who started out with menial jobs while they pursued their dreams. Madonna once had to survive by selling doughnuts in a Times Square shop. James Earl Jones once waxed floors for a living. Jerry Seinfeld sold light bulbs over the phone and fake jewelry on the street. Best-selling author Norman Vincent Peale wrote *The Power of Positive Thinking* in his fifties. He submitted the manuscript to many publishers, but was rejected many times. He became so dejected that he finally threw his manuscript in the trash can and forbade his wife from removing it. She did not remove it, but brought it to him the next day in the trash can and encouraged him to keep submitting it. The book was eventually picked up by a publisher and has since sold twenty million copies in forty-two languages around the world! Norman Vincent Peale went on to found the magazine *Guideposts*, which sells millions of copies every year. J.K. Rowling, the author of the wildly successful *Harry Potter* series, was a single mother on welfare when she wrote her first book. Now she is richer than the Queen of England. None of these people were destined to succeed until they made a *firm* decision to follow their passion no matter what. They put intangibles over tangibles.

What's the difference between these people and you? Right now, wherever you are, whatever you're doing, you have everything within you that you need to succeed. You just have to reach down deeper than you've ever reached before and find it. You have to work harder than you've ever worked and sacrifice more than ever before in order to get where you want to be. Success comes when you follow your passion. This is the only way to truly succeed. Life is too short to waste it on things you don't enjoy and that lack meaning for you. But it all starts with a decision — a decision between tangibles and intangibles. This is the decision behind the decision.

When you move in the direction of your dreams, unseen spiritual forces move too. Author and photographer James Balog explains what artists from ancient times to the present have always known:

> "Spectacular images, I have long been convinced, are destined to come into being. Perhaps it's no more complicated than working hard, pushing endlessly to be in the right place at the right time, and making your own luck. Maybe it's a matter of being receptive to a "happy accident," the kind of thing that artists in other media actively court and that can lead to an

epiphany: the seemingly stray splash of paint on a canvas, or the random crack in a sculptor's block of granite. Or it may be the influence of what the ancient Greeks called the Muses, superhuman forces molding life experience into the creative form it was ultimately meant to assume.

I love the philosophy that you have to work hard to create your own luck. In order to see an eagle fly, you have to go to where eagles fly. In order to watch sea turtles hatch out of the sand and run to the sea, you have to go to where sea turtles nest. In order to feel the mist of the spray from the spout of a whale, you have to go to where whales play. Epiphany, enlightenment, and insight do not happen as randomly as we think. You have to go to where they are most likely to happen. And the more you expect the unexpected, the more often the unexpected seems to happen. When you move, unseen spiritual forces rise up to meet you, to make your dreams happen.

Author Marsha Sinetar wrote a book entitled *Do What You Love, The Money Will Follow.* In it she teaches that pursuing your passion is the only way to find true success. When you do this, the financial rewards eventually follow. But remember that your success is not measured by how much money you earn pursuing your passion, but by the fact that you have liberated yourself to do what you love. This is the law of the harvest. You will ultimately reap what you sow. You must plant the seeds today of the fruit that you want to enjoy tomorrow or it will never come. What kind of seeds are you planting today? Will it yield the kind of fruit you want to eat one day? Will it yield the kind of fruit you will be proud to have spent the bulk of your life nurturing and harvesting? I have several friends who have given up their careers to become full-time artists. They live on next to nothing and have to live with family or friends to make ends meet. But they are following their dreams. They have chosen intangibles over tangibles. They are following their passion. They may not be famous yet, but they are happy and fulfilled. They place more value on intangibles than on tangibles.

How many people do you know who would like to go to Africa for a vacation? How many people do you know who would like to play with lion cubs and leopard cubs for a living? I have a friend who is an apartment manager and loves animals. When I showed her pictures of myself playing with lion cubs in Africa, she cried. She would love to work with animals for a living, but this dream seems too far off and difficult for her. As a result, she is doing absolutely nothing to pursue this dream. It's easy to see how this is a self-fulfilling prophecy. She believes she can't. Therefore, she is unwilling to invest any time and effort in it. Her failure to be proactive guarantees that she will never fulfill her dream.

I have another friend, Caily Ermer, who lives in Africa and works at a game lodge. She plays with lion cubs for a living and takes people on drives of the African savannah to see all types of wildlife. She is also a photographer. All her life she dreamed of doing this. She worked hard to obtain a zoology degree in England and then started applying for jobs in Africa. She finally landed this job at a game lodge where they give her room and board and a small salary. She is not making a lot of money, and she will never become wealthy doing what she is doing now. But she is living her dream. She has chosen to put intangibles over tangibles.

The point is that dreaming and visualization are meaningless if you are not willing to take specific action designed to bring you closer to your dream. These two women are exactly the same age. One worked hard to achieve her dreams and is currently living them. The other is still dreaming.

The issue of focusing on intangible values also raises the issue of choosing between relationships and career. Many of the professional women I know sooner or later have faced the question of whether to take time off from work to have children (the "mommy track"), or to take the "fast track" toward career advancement. This is a huge decision for many women who pride themselves on their career accomplishments thus far and still have more that they want to achieve. The choice is between ambition and family. Some of the most talented and ambitious female attorneys I have known have decided to quit the practice of law altogether in order to raise children. Why would they do this? These were women who swore in the beginning that nothing would come between them and their career goals. But when the children came, they listened to their hearts, and their love for their children won out. There is something incredibly wonderful about holding a child to which you have given life and knowing that it depends solely on you for love, support, and its very survival. When a mother looks into the eyes of her newborn baby and strokes its downy soft cheeks, everything else fades into oblivion. It does so even for fathers.

Around nine years ago, I was faced with a choice between a promotion to my company's headquarters in another city, which would have tremendously benefited my career, and staying in Austin so I could be near my children, who were living with their mother at that time. Staying in Austin narrowed my career options and was going to mean working for a small boutique litigation firm with less security. But it would keep me in Austin near my children. At the time, my two little girls were six and eight years old. For me there was only one choice.

I recorded the reasons for my decision in my journal as follows:

- *Relationships give life meaning.* They define who we are. They are the purpose behind every purpose we pursue. What is the use of achieving a difficult goal if you have no one to share in your joy? Anything you enjoy alone is twice as satisfying when you enjoy it with someone else.

- *Treasure your friends and your family above all else.* For when everything else is gone — money, houses, land, fortune, and fame — this is all you really have left. A strong friend can carry you through any crisis or tragedy. But if you are alone when tragedy strikes, you have to endure the pain of the tragedy itself plus the tragedy of being alone. Two people who love and respect each other can endure any pain, if they endure it together.

- *He who betrays his best friend is not worthy of future friends.* He will be betrayed himself and he will suffer alone.

- *If we are to leave any legacy at all, we leave it only in the hearts and minds of those to whom we have showed love and kindness during our lifetime.* Those whose lives have been imprinted with our own will bear a piece of our soul in their hearts forever. Their way of thinking, their outlook on life, or the very course of their life may have been forever altered because of our influence.

■ *The impact we have on the lives of others is our only true legacy.* This is the only thing that truly lasts when we are gone. Let us be careful to walk softly and gently through the sands of other people's lives. The footprints we leave behind will be there forever. Treasure relationships above all else. For this is all we really have.

Needless to say, I chose to stay in Austin, near my kids. The unexpected surprise was that less than two years later, I won an $18 million verdict with that little boutique firm on a case I never would have handled had I chosen to take the company's promotion and move to another city. But the real treasure was the time I got to spend with my kids that I would have forfeited had I left.

Whatever obstacle you are facing, take a step back and consider whether there is an intangible solution that could help. I am not an idealist. I do not advocate that simply thinking about, praying about, or meditating about a problem will make it go away. Action and hard work are necessary.

As a courtroom litigator, I have represented both plaintiffs and defendants in both tiny cases and multimillion-dollar cases. Yet, over the years I have come to learn that there is in an intangible solution to almost every legal dispute, which few people recognize and even fewer people apply. Every courtroom litigator knows that the same four things drive almost every lawsuit. Those four things are anger, pride, revenge, and greed — on both sides of the dispute. Money is only symbolic of these intangibles and has become a way to measure success. Lawsuits are resolved when people are finally able to let go of these things and make objective economic decisions based on a true cost/benefit analysis. This may sound simplistic, but the statistics show that in almost all lawsuits, the only people who come out ahead are the lawyers. The "winner" is deemed to be the party that has lost the least amount of blood in the fight.

But what about those who win multimillion-dollar verdicts? On May 26, 2000, at Lake Worth Middle School in West Palm Beach, Florida, a 13-year-old boy shot his English teacher, Barry Grunow, with a .25 caliber handgun he had stolen from a family friend. The boy was caught, tried, and convicted; and was sentenced to twenty-eight years in prison. Two years later, the widow, Pam Grunow won a lawsuit, not against the murderer or his family, but against the "deep pockets." The court awarded her $18 million from the family friend from whom the murderer had stolen the gun, $12 million from the school board, and $1.2 million from Valor Corporation, the distributor of the gun. Wasn't this lawsuit justified?

Yes, but what purpose did it serve to award this much money to *just one* person? Can any amount of money bring back our deceased loved ones? Will giving all this money to *one person* in Florida really serve as a deterrent to prevent students from killing their teachers all over the country? What was really driving this lawsuit? Was it greed? Was it anger? Was it revenge?

Aren't there any *intangible* solutions to the problem of kids shooting their teachers? How about better upbringing? How about discipline? How about character training in public schools? How about not letting our kids watch thousands of murders day in and day out on TV and at theaters (solely for the purpose of entertainment!) to the point where they become desensitized?

At the time of this writing, the latest breaking news is that a high school kid named Jeff Weiss shot both his grandparents and then went on a shooting spree at Red Lake High School in Minnesota that left seven more dead and fifteen wounded. What could possibly be driving this kind of behavior?

A gun is a tool, like a hammer. It is neither evil nor good in and of itself. It is neutral. You can use the hammer to build a house or you can use it to bash someone over the head. In the 1800's, it was perfectly legal for a 13-year-old kid to carry a handgun. But I don't remember any historical evidence that there was a problem with 13-year-olds shooting their teachers or *each other* at school. Have guns become any more dangerous today than they were 150 years ago? Or is it *we* who have become more dangerous?

The bottom line is that there are intangible solutions to most of the world's tangible problems if we will just look for them and apply them. The Enron scandal is the worst scandal (so far) in the 21st century. Rebecca Smith and John R. Emshwiller were the two *Wall Street Journal* reporters who uncovered the corruption within Enron. They have written a wonderful book called *24 Days*, explaining, day by day, how they unraveled the fraud. In the last chapter of the book, they make a brilliant observation about what caused

Enron to fall. They concluded that what really toppled Enron was "greed, ambition, and pride." Intangibles are more important than tangibles.

What about family disputes, crime on the streets, economic problems, pollution, marital problems, and the like? I am no genius, but it seems to me that the solutions just might be discipline, forgiveness, honesty, responsibility, commitment, humility, generosity, sacrifice, diligence, cleanliness, acceptance, courtesy, selflessness, creativity, cooperation, and understanding.

Granted, if all of these intangible solutions fail, there may be no choice but to take hard, swift action and press on with the fight — even if it means fighting to the death. I believe this was the case in the American Colonies' fight for independence and in America's decision to join World War II. The problem is that most of us don't take time to look to see if an intangible solution exists that might resolve the problem before we fight. True heroes see the intangible solutions that no one else sees.

THE DECISION BEHIND THE DECISION:
**Heroes CHOOSE to put intangible values
above all else.**

HEROES CAN SEE WHAT'S TRULY SACRED AND WHAT'S NOT

*"To give pleasure to a single heart by a single act
is better than a thousand heads bowing in prayer."*
— GANDHI

Most people think of *The Adventures of Huckleberry Finn* by Mark Twain as a fun adventure story. But if you look beneath the surface, it teaches some profound lessons. In the story, Huckleberry Finn and the runaway slave Jim become best friends as they both live a life on the run. They spend their days on a handmade raft on the lazy Mississippi River. Huck is on the run from his relatives, who want to "civilize him" after his alcoholic father has died. Jim is in search of his freedom and the privilege of buying his family back from their slave owners. They are both rebels on the run.

One day while Jim is sleeping on the raft, Huck begins feeling guilty about helping him escape from his owner, who was a friend of his family's back home. He has been taught that it is a sin to steal another's "property" and that it is even worse to help a slave escape. He begins to realize that he will probably go to hell for this unless he turns Jim in to his proper owner. Feeling guilty, Huck writes a letter to Jim's owner revealing his whereabouts and plans to send the letter as soon as he can. But then he begins to daydream. He remembers all the good times he and Jim have had along the way. He remembers how Jim has done so much for him and how Jim sacrificed his own safety for Huck. He is struggling with the biggest decision of his very young life, caught between his love for his best friend and what his society had taught him was right and wrong.

According to the religious beliefs he grew up with, Huck was choosing between heaven and hell. He believed if he did not turn in his friend, he would go to hell. The climax comes when he looks at his friend sleeping peacefully, looks at the letter, and then says, "All right then, I'll go to hell." He tears up the note and throws it in the river. What a moral victory! What a triumph! In his childlike innocence, Huck Finn teaches us great wisdom. What he had been taught was right and wrong turned out to be the opposite of what was actually right and wrong. He followed his heart in the face of great opposition. In his heart, he knew he had done the right thing.

In Huckleberry Finn's mind, he was going to hell. But he was willing to do it for his friend. As we know, Huck's decision ultimately proves to be the higher way. The religious beliefs taught by his society would later be condemned. But how was Huck to know this as such a young man struggling with this big decision? He thought he was going to hell.

Billions of people, including myself, look for spiritual guidance when faced with serious problems. But sometimes what we believe to be divine influence is just a product of our upbringing or education. The lesson to be learned from the Huckleberry Finn story is: "Don't check your mind at the door of a difficult decision." You have a God-given ability to know right from wrong. Like Huck Finn, your own heart and your own instincts may turn out to be right. The conventional wisdom of your spiritual leaders may not be right for you. Never rely solely on what someone else tells you is God's will for your life or that something is meant to be. How do you know when it is an all-knowing spiritual force guiding you? How do you know it's not your own feelings or desires, or worse yet, the desires and interests of another person influencing you?

We know from history that it's easy for people to claim something is God's will if they want it badly enough. Remember, we tend to see what we're *expecting* to see. If this is true when it comes to physical objects, is it even more true when it comes to the spiritual world? We know from history that priests, rabbis, pastors, and gurus don't always get it right. We know that humans have justified many atrocities over the centuries in God's name for their own personal gain. The fact is that no one has a monopoly on what is divine. The frightening thing is that, instead of taking control of our own lives, many of us would still rather rely on religious leaders for our sense of right and wrong, our sense of self-worth, and guidance in making tough decisions.

It's all too common these days to hear of a cult leader who has persuaded his followers to sell all they have, to give their money to him, to give him their wives and daughters for sexual pleasure, and to live apart from the rest of society. It's shocking to know that there are still people out there who will continue to be taken in by these supposed spiritual leaders. Jim Jones (who made his followers drink arsenic in a cup of fruit punch), Marshall Applewhite (of the Heaven's

Gate cult), and David Koresh (who led the Branch Davidians in Waco, Texas) were all disillusioned and charismatic leaders who led people to their deaths. But what was it about their followers' thought processes that prevented them from distinguishing between reality and what their leaders were teaching them? What was it that stopped them from saying, "Hey! Why are they doing this?"

> *"Do not believe what you have heard. Do not believe in tradition because it is handed down by many genera-tions. Do not believe in anything that has been spoken of many times. Do not believe because the written statements come from some old sage. Do not believe in conjecture. Do not believe in authority or teachers or elders. But after careful observation and analysis, when it agrees with reason and it will benefit one and all, then accept it and live by it."*
>
> — BUDDHA

When you accept the fact that you don't need spiritual advisors to tell you what God thinks is right or wrong, you will be truly enlightened and you will see things you never saw before. Martin Luther, the 15th-century German monk who challenged the religious leaders of his day, is a perfect example of what can happen when we do our own research and rely on our own judgment. In 1517 Martin Luther post-ed his *Ninety-Five Theses* at the Wittenberg Church, protest-ing the sale of forgiveness by the Church and exposing the lie that human beings needed organized religion to get to God. By this one simple act, Martin Luther single-handedly started the Reformation, out of which eventually flowed the funda-mental belief in the individual rights of man that prevails today. Martin Luther made a tough decision, but he was willing to face the consequences.

He was excommunicated by Pope Leo X and condemned as a heretic by Emperor Charles V. Yet at his trial, referred to as the Diet of Worms, Luther explained the basis of his decision to defend himself rather than recant. Luther counted the cost and made his decision based on what he believed was right. At his trial, Luther stated:

> "What I have just said I think will clearly show that I have well considered and weighed the dangers to which I am exposing myself ... I neither can nor will retract anything; for it cannot be right for a Christian to speak against his conscience. Here I stand; I cannot do otherwise. God help me. Amen."

A monument to Luther now bears the words, *"Hier steh ich, ich kann nicht anders,"* which loosely translated means, "I stand here and can do no more." Luther was considered a rebel, but he followed his heart and it changed the course of history. The decision behind his decision was to stick to what he knew was right despite the consequences. Luther made this decision because he saw something only heroes can see. He saw something truly sacred and he was willing to suffer for it. He saw the truth.

Christopher Columbus, who challenged the prevailing view that the world was flat, is another example of the benefits of creative individual thought. His willingness to pursue truth in the face of religious opposition literally opened up a "New World." But Christopher Columbus wasn't just pursuing a physical New World. He was pursuing something far greater. He was pursuing the truth and that's what made him a hero.

Galileo is another classic example. In 1633, when the prevailing view was that the earth was the center of the universe, the Roman Catholic Church condemned Galileo for teaching that the earth went around the sun. In its indictment of Galileo, the Church stated:

"The doctrine that the earth is neither the center of the universe nor immovable, but moves even with a daily rotation, is absurd, and both psychologically and theologically false, and at least an error of faith."

Threatened with torture, Galileo reluctantly recanted his teaching as being heresy on June 22, 1633. After Galileo formally recanted his position, he is reported to have said under his breath, *"e pur si muove,"* which means "but it does move." Now every year, the U.S. Supreme Court gives out a *"E Pur Si Muove"* award to the lower court judges who were the most vindicated judges of the year. Although Galileo proved to be right, it took the Catholic Church until 1992, *over three hundred years,* to formally repudiate its denunciation of Galileo.

Carl Sagan, in his book *Pale Blue Dot,* wisely asks, "Why were threats and Galileo's house arrest needed? Cannot truth defend itself in its confrontation with error?" In other words, if the truth is the truth, eventually it will reveal itself.

The truth does not need threats, intimidation, or social pressure to convince others of its validity. Einstein's theory of relativity was condemned by one hundred Nazi professors, but in the end Einstein was proven right. In response to the Nazi professors, Einstein simply stated, "If I were wrong, one professor would have been enough."

Dr. Gerald Mann, pastor of Riverbend Church in Austin, Texas, has stated, "The biggest of all the heresies is the belief that we can save God from heresies . . . God can defend himself." How big is God if he needs mere mortals to defend him from the heresies and misunderstandings of other mere mortals? The Scriptures tell us that our understanding of God pales in comparison to who he really is.

*"For now we see as though we were looking through
a foggy glass. But then we will see face to face."*
— I CORINTHIANS 13:12

In a speech in 1992, Pope John Paul II explained the reason for the Church's error regarding Galileo:

"The error of the theologians of the time, when they maintained the centrality of the earth, was to think that our understanding of the physical world's structure was in some way imposed by the literal sense of Sacred Scriptures."

In other words, the Pope acknowledged that it's not wise to put God in a box. The Scriptures are not a scientific analysis of how the physical world operates. Nor were they ever meant to be. There are many truths out there that we may not yet have discovered, both in the physical and spiritual realms. As we find bits of truth in the universe, we find bits of God. Who is man to claim he has a complete grasp of the ways of the universe, much less the ways of God?

*"For my ways are higher than your ways
and my thoughts than your thoughts."*
— ISAIAH 55:9

Remember that the greatest truths in life are seldom delivered by a booming voice from the clouds. Our guidance most often comes to us through trial and error, objective evidence, lessons we have learned along the way, and our own inner voice. Remember to pay attention to the lessons life is trying to teach you. The decision behind the decision is to think independently and be willing to rely on the objective evidence and your own instincts despite the pressures and forces that may oppose you. When you do this, your eyes will be opened just like the eyes of Martin Luther, Columbus, and Galileo, and you, like them, will see things you never saw before. You will see something truly sacred. You will see truth.

Don't wait for a voice from the clouds before you act. If you do, you will wait forever. Follow your instincts and desires. Follow your natural strengths. Your natural talents and interests exist for a reason. I believe the things that motivate us do not exist by accident. I believe the things we feel passionate about come from a divine pipeline to our heart. When we listen to our heart and follow our instincts, I believe we are tapping into what is truly divine.

> **THE DECISION BEHIND THE DECISION:**
> **Heroes CHOOSE to pursue truth above else.**

HEROES CAN SEE
THE "RIGHT PATH"

"The content of your character is your choice.
Day by day, what you choose, what you think,
and what you do is who you become.
Your integrity is your destiny . . .
it is the light that guides your way."

— HERACLITUS

Heroes have the ability to see the "right path" when everyone else sees "gray areas" and loopholes. We live in a world with millions of laws, codes, regulations, and ordinances. The tentacles of the law reach into every aspect of our lives including the cars we drive, what we watch on TV, what we listen to on the radio, what we see on the Internet, what we eat, what we drink, and even the air we breathe. Point out any item in your house, and I can tell you some body of law that probably affects it.

To understand the law you need a three-year law degree, and even then the best lawyers can only master one or two areas of law in a lifetime. The more laws we create, the more gray areas and loopholes we create.

For example, in Washington State, two men were indicted for photographing and videotaping women's privates under their skirts in public places. The jury convicted them of violating the state's law against voyeurism, which is designed to keep people "safe from hostile intrusion or surveillance." The case was appealed and the Supreme Court of Washington State reversed the convictions on the ground that, technically, the men had not violated any law. The voyeurism law didn't specifically say you could not take photographs and videotapes of women's privates underneath their skirts — as long as they were in public. Judge Bobbe Bridge wrote, "It is the physical location of the person that is ultimately at issue, not the part of the person's body." It so happened that the photographs and videotapes were taken at a public mall and an outdoor festival. This is a classic example of a loophole. There was a public outcry and immediately the legislature began drafting a new law to plug this loophole.

Okay, so we can't expect a couple of perverted renegades to exactly be looking for "the right path" to begin with. But what about ABC News? On ABCnews.com, there was a Real Player link to a video segment that showed what appears to be one of the "upskirt" shots. Did ABC use the photos of the victims to get attention and draw more viewers to its site? Was ABC just as guilty of invading the privacy of these women?

Of course, when the media does it, all kinds of First Amendment issues arise. If it's "newsworthy" it's okay, and anyone trying to stop it is accused of censorship, which is deemed unconstitutional and un-American. More loopholes.

Why do we need so many laws when a few simple rules should suffice? The easy ones that come to mind are don't kill, don't steal, don't lie, and don't cheat. You may be able to think of a few others. But if all laws were abolished and everyone in the world actually followed these simple rules, the world would be a much better place. The crime rate would be reduced to almost zero because there would be no deception, no cheating, no stealing, and no killing. There would be no war. There would be very few lawsuits. Most of us lawyers would be out of a job. Business would operate 100% more efficiently and profitably because people doing deals could be confident that they weren't being deceived, people would work an honest day's work for an honest day's pay, and manufacturers and retailers would produce only the safest and highest quality goods. Life isn't nearly as complicated as we think. Heroes have the ability to see the right path despite the "gray areas" and loopholes.

Granted, there are some questions out there for which there are no right or wrong answers. But they are few and far between. Moses and Zach were two teenage boys who were brothers. They lived for adventure. Together with their faithful dog Dakota, they would go camping, hiking, biking, fishing, hunting, and mountain climbing together. They were inseparable. They defended each other in all situations. One summer evening, they made a pact beneath the towering pecan tree they had spent all day jumping off of into a river. They swore that if the other was ever in an accident, or became so sick that he would spend the rest of his life in endless pain, or if his body was so badly damaged that he could not function, the other brother would somehow end his life out of mercy.

One day, as fate would have it, Moses was in a motorcycle accident that nearly ended his life. The surgeons worked for hours and managed to keep him breathing and his bodily functions working, but only with the aid of a life support system. He was in a coma, and it was unclear whether he would ever come out of it. After several months, the doctors told his family it was unlikely that he would ever come out of the coma. Zach had a tough decision to make. He had made a pact. Should he honor the pact he had made with Moses or not? Would anyone else understand?

After months of struggling with this decision, one day Zach went into Moses' hospital room and stared at all the tubes and wires protruding from what used to be his vibrant, laughing, athletic brother. As he remembered all the good times they had together, Zach began to weep. His mind took him back to the banks of the river under the big pecan tree they had jumped from into the water. It was under this tree that they had made their pact. With Dakota and God as their only witnesses, they had made their pact.

Zach went to the main plug that controlled the breathing apparatus pumping oxygen into his brother's lungs and stood there for a moment. Finally, he slowly but deliberately pulled the plug. The machine turned off, and Moses quit breathing. After a few moments, Moses was dead. A nurse entered the room and saw Zach leaning over his brother, crying like a baby. The monitors showed no heartbeat and no brain waves. The nurse noticed that the breathing apparatus wasn't working. Frantically running around trying to see what had gone wrong, the nurse finally noticed that the cord wasn't plugged in.

Ultimately, Zach was indicted for murder. Here is your morality test question: If you were on the jury in the trial of this boy, would you vote to convict or acquit? Ask your friends and neighbors what they would do. See what kind of reactions you get. The Academy Award-winning movie *Million*

Dollar Baby, with Clint Eastwood and Hilary Swank, presented us with this same dilemma.

The real life question of whether to turn off Terri Schiavo's feeding tubes dominated the headlines for weeks during the Spring of 2005. A lower court authorized her husband to turn off the feeding tubes, and the U.S. Supreme Court refused to intervene. Some called it murder. Others called it mercy. After that, millions of people searched the internet for forms on how to create a "living will" so that their families would be authorized to "pull the plug."

Even the most honest and ethical person in the world doesn't always know what the "right" thing is. The right thing according to whom? The right thing in what circumstances? Where do you go for guidance? Who do you ask? What factors do you consider when you're faced with a moral or ethical dilemma? Do you follow the Golden Rule — *Do unto others as you would have them do unto you?* Do you conduct a cost/benefit analysis? Do you consider only the *tangible* costs and benefits of doing what you are considering, or do you also consider the *intangible* costs and benefits? Are the real-world consequences of doing what you are considering worth whatever benefits you think you will obtain?

When we are under extreme pressure, our judgment-making ability is often impaired. When we are faced with a crisis, we may be tempted to fudge a little, to lie a little, to cheat a little, to destroy someone's character a little. But this usually complicates the issue and only creates bigger obstacles than the original crisis we were facing. I have represented more than one client who was in this exact situation.

Stop and think about it. From a tangible cost/benefit analysis, some of the relevant questions are: What if my spouse and family knew? What if I am caught? What if my boss finds out? Remember, if you can't live with the consequences of the worst case scenario, you should not seriously consider this option. Tragedy happens in the decision-making process when we ignore or discount real-world possibilities. When bells and whistles go off and red flags are raised in your head, it is time to pay attention. Don't sleepwalk through the decision making process.

When dealing with moral and ethical choices, the cost/benefit analysis is usually much more intangible and subjective than in other decisions. It raises questions such as: Could I live with myself if I did this? Could I recommend this as the best course of action if my children came to me for advice? Could I announce publicly what I did without shame? Would my mother be proud of me?

What do you do when the cashier gives you too much change back? What if you find a wallet with money in it? What do you consider to be an appropriate tax deduction? These questions all stem from moral and ethical situations we find ourselves in from time to time. There are countless others. How we deal with these situations reveals a great deal about who we are.

The process of decision making when dealing with moral and ethical choices is very personal and private. Usually when we are tempted, it is in a situation in which we believe that "no one will ever find out." Therefore, we are not likely to consult mentors or seek advice from friends, family, or spiritual leaders. Our conscience is our only guide. The true test of a person's character is how he acts when he thinks no one is watching.

This chapter cannot tell you what decision to make when faced with any particular moral or ethical choice. Only you know your particular circumstances. Only you can weigh the spiritual and tangible factors related to your options. This chapter is not designed to teach you the difference between right and wrong. Your family, your church or temple, your schools, and your life experiences all should have prepared you for the moral and ethical choices you will face in life. This chapter is designed only to encourage you to make principled decisions and to help you explore the various factors you should consider when faced with a tough moral or ethical choice.

One of the first things my instructors tried to teach me in law school was that there is no sanctity to any contract. According to my contracts professor, the parties to a contract do not owe any ethical or moral duty to each other to keep their word. I was taught that contractual promises do not involve morality. They are amoral. The parties to a contract have only promised they will abide by the contract or suffer the legal and economic consequences if they fail to do so. Thus, if there is ever a scenario where one person finds it more profitable to break the contract than to keep it, this professor taught that this person is perfectly justified in breaking it. It is not a crime to do so. According to my contracts professor, questions of morality are not relevant. There is only a tangible cost/benefit analysis. I have seen too many big companies operate according to this principle — with tragic results.

I happen to disagree with this philosophy. Any philosophy that places greater emphasis on maximizing profit at all costs than on principles of right and wrong is doomed to failure. But, of course, before you can even have a moral dilemma, you have to have morals. Before you can make the external choice, you have to make the internal choice to live according to certain principles. This is the decision behind the decision.

You have to choose integrity over convenience. When corporations and executives make decisions in their ivory towers, sheltered from the realities of the daily lives of their workers, they often have to choose between maximizing profits and what is best for their employees. Maximizing profits by reducing costs, when taken to an extreme, can result in frustrated employees who are expected to achieve outstanding results with little or no resources. When I was corporate counsel to a Fortune 500 company, I saw this firsthand. Forcing frustrated employees to work with few resources can result in shoddy workmanship and the production of dangerously defective products, which can lead to multimillion dollar litigation. Such multimillion dollar litigation has led to the failure of many corporations.

We can encourage people to follow the "right path," but we can't teach a corporation to do so. Corporations are not people. They have no soul and no conscience. Yet the U.S. laws treat corporations as though they are real people, and give them the same protections as real people. The U.S. laws assume corporations will use judgment and discretion which, by definition, they do not have. This can result in corporations making decisions that are technically legal but ethically wrong. When this happens, society is harmed.

For example, most people don't realize that many of the devices Enron used to deceive the public were technically legal because they complied with what are known as "generally accepted accounting principles." Generally accepted accounting principles are the customs and standards adopted by the accounting industry; they are designed to make sure everyone can read everyone else's balance sheets and income statements consistently. But they allow "judgment" and "discretion" about *how* and *when* to account for certain items, such as income and expenses, and also *what counts* as income and *what counts* as an expense.

More significantly, under federal law, only *"material"* misstatements and omissions are considered fraudulent. What does that mean? The *Texas Journal of Business Law* says: "A numerical rule of thumb has emerged — misstatements of less than five percent are not material" (Vol. 39, No. 2, Fall 2003, Matthew S. Mokwa). Basically that means that we've been allowing our corporate giants, whose gross income is larger than some countries, to lie "a little," to cheat "a little," and to steal "a little" for a very long time. Where Enron went wrong was that it crossed the line. It lied, cheated, and stole "too much." Enron used "creative accounting" to hide billions of dollars of debt and to create the illusion of billions of dollars of income. When the fraud was exposed, the stock became worthless, the company filed bankruptcy, and the life savings of thousands of employees evaporated. The answer from Congress was to pass the Sarbanes-Oxley Act, which was designed to plug the loopholes. More laws.

When faced with the choice between maximizing profits and doing what is "right," take into account the long-term ramifications on your personal reputation, the reputation of your business, and potential litigation costs, as well as the mental and emotional costs to you and your employees. Simply put, when you are faced with a moral dilemma, you are not just dealing with fuzzy concepts of right and wrong; your decisions have real-world consequences that can affect you and other people permanently. Despite the size of the

Enron scandal, there were a few heroes within the company who saw what the company was doing and spoke out against it at the expense of their jobs.

When we attempt to expose fraud, we sometimes become the next victim. This is what happened in the multimillion-dollar lawsuit *Food Lion v. ABC PrimeTime.* In that case, former employees of Food Lion accused the store of food mishandling practices and fraudulent food dating, endangering the health of customers. As part of an investigation, several undercover ABC employees applied for and received jobs in various food handling sections of a Food Lion store. They lied about their employment histories in order to get hired. While employed by Food Lion, they secretly videotaped employees deliberately training other employees how to mix old, outdated food with fresh food, how to re-label packaged food to conceal the fact that it was out of date, and other similar "cost-saving" practices. ABC aired the footage of these videotapes nationally on *PrimeTime* and Food Lion subsequently lost millions of dollars in sales. Food Lion cried foul and sued ABC for the secret manner it used to obtain the story. However, the videotapes spoke for themselves.

This story presents two different sets of moral and ethical decisions. The first issue involves the question: To what lengths should the press be allowed to go in order to expose illegal activity? The second involves the extent to which businesses should be allowed to cut costs and maximize profits. Is it worth risking human lives for the sake of the almighty dollar? This shouldn't be a tough decision.

Due to some smart trial strategies by the Food Lion attorneys, the only issue the jury was allowed to address was whether ABC had acted properly, not whether Food Lion's food handling employees had acted properly. At the trial, little or no evidence was presented regarding Food Lion's food handling practices. Therefore, the jury never focused on whether Food Lion was guilty of gross food mishandling practices. Without all the facts and after having heard only one side of the story, the jury sided with Food Lion and awarded it $5.5 million in punitive damages. Thus, the good that ABC was attempting to accomplish was punished, while the propriety of Food Lion's food handling practices was ignored in the courtroom. A skewed verdict was the result.

A *Nightline* debate was subsequently held at Wake Forrest University between ABC representatives and Food Lion executives, with students and professors in the audience asking questions. ABC defended its practices by giving examples of all the good it had done and all the human suffering it had stopped over the years by exposing improper and inhumane business practices on national television. ABC in essence argued that deceit in pursuit of a just cause is sometimes justifiable. Food Lion executives waved the banner that deceit is always wrong no matter what the purpose. Never mind that Food Lion had been accused of deceiving its own customers and endangering their health for financial gain. They also relied heavily on the fact that ABC had never "technically" proven that Food Lion had ever done anything wrong.

The dispute can be distilled to this question: When, if ever, does the end justify the means? Some moral choices that should be easy are sometimes difficult, depending on the circumstances.

During the debate, an ABC representative asked a Food Lion executive whether it would be proper for someone to lie in order to become a Nazi guard at a death camp for the purpose of secretly filming the atrocities of the Holocaust. The Food Lion executive responded that it was unfair to compare the Holocaust to outdated potato salad. But he never answered the question.

The legal and ethical issue underlying the Food Lion case has far-reaching ramifications on the question of when the end justifies the means. This fundamental issue may one day reach the U.S. Supreme Court. But I do not believe that the Court is qualified to answer it.

My personal view is that there is no absolute answer to this question. Rather, there is a continuum or a sliding scale in which the answer varies depending on the facts of each case. In some instances, if the atrocity we are trying to expose and abolish is extremely heinous, then humanity would most likely vindicate the decision to abolish the evil by any means available, legal or illegal. The Holocaust is a good example. Whatever it took, the extermination of six million Jews should have been stopped. Humanity would have vindicated the person or the army who stopped this atrocity regardless of the means used.

In contrast, we would not want to use a bazooka to kill a mouse. Some measures may be improper if the means used are extreme compared to the "evil" we are trying to eradicate. I believe it is wrong to cut off someone's hand for stealing an apple, even if you are trying to send a message to other apple thieves. Some minor wrongs in the world may go uncorrected, but the greater good of society is achieved by using only extreme measures to correct the most severe wrongs.

The question is, who makes this judgment call? Where do we draw the line? Should elected judges, who are subject to being influenced by political affiliations and campaign funds, draw the line? Should randomly selected jurors, who have no knowledge of the law and who naturally bring in their own biases, draw the line? Should state legislatures or the federal government draw the line?

In America, we tend to favor the rights of the individual over the rights of society. For example, the courts have determined that the Fourth Amendment of the U.S. Constitution protects our right to privacy even when the government has good intentions, such as capturing a criminal. Before the police can search your house, they must have a search warrant which is supported by sworn testimony. This is good for your privacy and the result is that we don't have police kicking in our doors any time they want. But on occasion, a criminal or two may escape.

There is no single black-and-white test that can be applied to all situations. The answer depends on the facts of each case. Every day, all across the country, defense attorneys file motions to suppress evidence they claim was illegally obtained by the police in violation of the Fourth Amendment. This forces judges to look at the facts of each specific case individually to determine whether the police "crossed the line" in the measures they used to obtain the evidence. There is no single correct answer that applies in all instances. Sometimes the police follow the rules and sometimes they don't. Sometimes the best evidence that could be used to prove guilt is excluded from the courtroom because the police obtained it in an illegal manner. Then again, sometimes the police follow the rules, but the trial judge (who is only human) rules incorrectly and criminals go free. Our laws are made, interpreted, and enforced by humans, who are imperfect by nature.

The bottom line is that just because the courts or the legislature declare something legal or illegal doesn't necessarily make it right or wrong. Ethical and moral choices go to the very heart of mankind. Remember, no matter which government is in power or what that government says is right or wrong, you still have to live with yourself. Just because the rape and murder of Jews in Germany and Poland was generally accepted didn't make it right. Until recently, many people in South Africa and many corporations around the world generally accepted South Africa's government-sponsored segregation of blacks and whites. Not until 1994 did the government-sponsored doctrine of apartheid end in South Africa. But just because it was considered legal for many years under the Afrikaans-led government did not make apartheid morally right. Heroes are able to see the right path no matter what the government says is right or wrong.

No matter what the majority of people around you say, you still have a choice. You still have a legacy to leave for your children and grandchildren, your friends and relatives. What will your legacy be? These decisions reveal who you are more than any other decision you will ever make. If you have wronged someone, it is not too late to own up to it and work toward reconciliation.

THE DECISION BEHIND THE DECISION:
Heroes CHOOSE to live by a set of principles
that are not dependent on what the
government says is right or wrong.

HEROES SEE THE PAST DIFFERENTLY THAN MOST

"I am not discouraged, because every wrong attempt discarded is another step forward."

— THOMAS EDISON

Okay, sometimes we make mistakes. But mistakes can either work for us or against us. Our past mistakes can either paralyze us with guilt, or the fear of making more mistakes, or they can propel us forward. Heroes become heroes because they look at the past differently than most.

Can you guess why the household cleaner Formula 409 was given that name? I'll give you 408 guesses. That's right, it was the 409th formula the manufacturer tried that gave its chemists the results they wanted. What meaning was given to the first 408 tries? The meaning was that they had eliminated at least that many formulas that did not work. That gave them the motivation to keep trying.

What you accomplish in your future depends on how you have *decided* to view your past. How you interpret your past is a choice that you make, perhaps unconsciously. Take *conscious* control of how you view your past, and you will change your future forever.

When Edison experimented with electricity, he could have looked at his many unsuccessful experiments as failures. But he chose to look at them as successes because he knew that the more improper methods he got out of the way, the closer he would come to the formula that would ultimately succeed.

We tend to view decisions that don't give us the results we want as "mistakes" or "wrong" choices. But, to call something a mistake or a wrong choice is to cast judgment. If you think about it, in reality, there are only two things in life: cause and effect. For every cause, there is an effect. Sometimes we like the results we get; sometimes we don't. The point is to learn what caused the results we don't like and to adjust our behavior until we start getting the results we do like.

"In science, mistakes always precede the truth."
— HORACE WALPOLE

Consider the beautiful light display in the northern skies known as the *aurora borealis*, or the Northern Lights. Imagine ancient man staring at these lights one dark winter night. He doesn't know what to think, so he asks, "Why?" When no answer is readily apparent, he imagines the gods are dancing in the night or perhaps playing with fire. What he imagines the Northern Lights to be becomes reality to him. To other cultures in the area, the gods might be angry and demanding a virgin sacrifice. They would, therefore, act on what they imagine to be reality and perhaps a young girl would lose her life. To a Greek philosopher, the Northern Lights might raise questions regarding the meaning of life. To a writer, the Northern Lights might be inspiration for a poem. To a rabbi or minister, they might represent the glory of God. To an artist, the Northern Lights might represent breathtaking beauty to behold. To a scientist, they might represent energy particles from the sun colliding with oxygen and nitrogen particles in the earth's atmosphere to create small bursts of light called photons. You see, life and all that it consists of has only the significance that we give it. In the example of the Northern Lights, what we imagine them to be becomes our reality. Once we *choose* what to believe, it is natural to act in accordance with that belief. The most important choice then is choosing *what* we believe.

Every "mistake" we experience in life has only the significance we give it. What we *choose* to believe about our past actions has a huge impact on our self-image. Our feelings of worthiness and confidence determine what we are willing to try in the future.

Has it occurred to you that humans are the only animals that ask the question "Why?" Man has an unquenchable desire to understand *why* so that he can attach significance to events and judge their importance in his life. When the answers aren't readily apparent, we make up our own answers. It is sometimes easier to believe that the reason we did not succeed is because we are a "failure" rather than to do the substantive review and investigation required to determine exactly *why* we failed, and try again. We have the power and freedom to *choose* to believe we are a failure or to take the time and effort to figure out what went wrong and fix it.

But, as with Thomas Edison, just because you failed in the past doesn't mean you're a failure. Just because you did something bad in the past doesn't make you a bad person. Every day you can make the choice to take what you've learned and start over.

Every bad choice is an opportunity to learn. But we have to make a *decision* to learn from it. What are you telling yourself about the significant events in your life? What are you telling yourself about past "bad" decisions you've made? Have you convinced yourself that only a fool would have done what you did? Have you convinced yourself that you brought on your own suffering and deserved what you got? Are you painting past decisions with dark, dismal colors in your mind? Have you looked for the mixed blessings that came out of what you did?

> *"If you are distressed by anything external, the pain is not due to the thing itself, but to your estimate of it; and this you have the power to revoke at any moment."*
>
> — MARCUS AURELIUS

In order to learn from your mistakes, ask yourself why you made the decision you made. Retrace your mental and emotional processes. What factors were influencing you at the time? What set of criteria were you using to evaluate your options?

I have heard many people explain why they slept with other people against their better judgment and then felt bad about it later. The consistent theme is that they were lonely at the time and were looking for companionship, or they were depressed and needed whatever comfort they could find. If you can identify the reasons for why you do the things you do, the thing inside that motivates you, then you can identify the real source of the problem. Once you have identified the true source, you can find healthy ways to deal with the problem.

What motivated Martha Stewart to dump about $228,000 worth in ImClone Systems stock illegally? She was motivated by her desire to avoid approximately $51,000 in losses from the reduction in the stock's value, which she knew was about to happen the next day. For a woman who was a multimillionaire, was saving a mere $51,000 worth the public humiliation, attorney's fees, and jail time? What caused Clinton to lie to the nation about his affair with Monica Lewinsky when the story first broke in the Paula Jones litigation? It was his desire to avoid public embarrassment, shame, and humiliation. But, just as with Martha Stewart's stock scandal, the cover-up was worse than the crime. Clinton was not impeached for having an affair with an intern, he was impeached for perjury and obstruction of justice.

Figuring out why you do certain things is helpful if you're going to alter your behavior. When you come to understand how and why you made certain decisions in the past, you can adjust the criteria you consider important in the future. When the criteria you consider to be important change, the way in which you make decisions will change. When you change the way you make decisions, your whole life will change.

Have you gleaned any learning from your mistakes in order to improve your overall life? You can paint your past mistakes with new meaning if you are willing to look at them in a new light. What you did may not have necessarily been a mistake at all. Life is a process of trial and error. There is only cause and effect. Remember, there are no mistakes or failures unless you interpret them as such. How you choose to view your "mistakes" is the decision behind the decision.

Has it ever occurred to you that in baseball an excellent hitter is someone who fails 70% of the time? That's right — an excellent hitter is a player with a .300 batting average. You have to keep swinging if you're ever going to hit the ball. If you're going to succeed at baseball, you have to assume you'll strike out some of the time. What if Babe Ruth quit every time he struck out? Ironically, Babe Ruth held records for the number of times he struck out as well as the number of home runs he hit. If you keep swinging hard enough and often enough, you can know with confidence that when you do connect with the ball, there's a good chance you'll knock it out of the ballpark.

"Everything I did in my life that was worthwhile,
I caught hell for."
— Chief Justice Earl Warren

If you quit after your first few failures, you'll never know the thrill of victory. When you quit, you deny yourself the lessons those failures could teach you — the very lessons that will bring you to your goal! You may have misunderstood the whole process of failure. When you quit, you guarantee the very thing you fear — *failure to achieve the goal.* Give yourself a fighting chance. Heroes keep stepping up to the plate. Heroes keep showing up for the battle. Keep learning, and keep applying what you learn to future situations. When you do this, you cannot help but ultimately succeed.

"Regret for things we did can be tempered by time;
it is regret for the things we did not do that is inconsolable."
— Sydney J. Harris

As Viktor Frankl firmly believed, "That which does not kill me makes me stronger." There is hope. If you've made mistakes or if you feel down, get up and keep going. You may have many more mistakes to get out of the way before you arrive at what will work. When you emerge victorious, you'll be a much stronger and wiser person for it. Be thankful for all of life's challenges. Be thankful even for the mistakes you've made.

> *"Far better it is to dare mighty things, to win glorious triumphs even though checkered by failure, than to rank with those poor spirits who neither enjoy nor suffer much because they live in the gray twilight that knows neither victory nor defeat."*
>
> — THEODORE ROOSEVELT

Remember, no decision in the past has as great an effect on your future as any decision you can make today. You can change your future by starting over right now and by changing the actions that brought about the results you didn't like.

> *"Whenever I make a bum decision,*
> *I just go out and make another."*
>
> — HARRY S. TRUMAN

If you keep a weekly schedule on a calendar, you know already that nothing has as great an effect on what happens next week as what you get done this week. What you failed to get done last week is irrelevant. It just puts more pressure on you to work harder this week. It's the same in life. Rather than focus on what you did or did not get done before, focus on what you can get done now so you can have a better future.

"The great thing in this world is not so much where we are, but in what direction we are moving."
— OLIVER WENDELL HOLMES

Are you willing to change your actions in the present in order to change your future? What amount of energy, commitment, and creativity are you willing to invest today in order to get what you want tomorrow? It's impossible to drive a car forward if you're constantly looking in the rearview mirror. For just a moment, imagine that it's now one year from today. Project yourself forward in time. A year from now, what will you wish you had gotten done today?

There's nothing wrong with falling down in the mud as long as you don't wallow in it and make it your home. Failure is a temporary and very transitory event. It's not a final resting place. Every day is a new day.

"Fall seven times; stand up eight."
— JAPANESE PROVERB

Remember, how you view your past is a *decision* you make. Make a conscious choice to interpret your past differently, and you will change your future forever.

THE DECISION BEHIND THE DECISION:
Heroes CHOOSE to reshape past failures into springboards for future success.

HEROES SEE THROUGH THE "SMOKE"

*"Without counsel purposes are disappointed,
but in the multitude of counselors they are established."*
— PROVERBS 15:22

H eroes can see opportunities that others don't, in part because of which experts they rely on. When you are faced with a critical choice that requires an expert opinion, how do you know which expert to rely on? A 1990 *Wall Street Journal* article reported that when it comes to the critical decision between having heart surgery or the less intrusive angioplasty, heart surgeons tend to recommend surgery and cardiologists tend to recommend drugs, angioplasty, lasers, and other remedies. Each remedy represents a different school of thought. The bottom line is that specialists view a patient's symptoms through the lens of their own training and tend to recommend only what they know.

If you were the patient and had gone to see a heart surgeon first, you might have come away thinking you needed heart surgery — a formidable thought. But who are you to argue with an expert, right? Then again, if you had gone to a cardiologist first, you might have come away thinking that an angioplasty and a change in your diet were all that was necessary. Tough choice. Heroes can see through the smoke of experts' biased statements in order to objectively weigh the options.

The great cyclist, Lance Armstrong, was faced with this kind of choice when he was told that his testicular cancer had spread to his brain. An oncologist in Houston, Texas, insisted that the only cure was aggressive chemotherapy treatments with Bleomycin. But this treatment would severely affect Armstrong's lungs and would guarantee that he could never compete in cycling again. In contrast, a brain surgeon in Indiana told him that brain surgery was an option and that if he chose this option, his lungs would not be affected. However, the thought of someone opening his skull and cutting into his brain didn't appeal to Armstrong either. Oncologists tend to recommend chemotherapy because that is what they know; brain surgeons tend to recommend brain surgery.

Because the cancer was spreading very quickly, Armstrong was forced to make an equally quick decision based on what each of the doctors had told him, and on his gut instinct. In his book *It's Not About the Bike*, he describes his dilemma as follows:

> "I had to choose my doctors and my place of treatment, and it wasn't like choosing a mutual fund either. If I invested in a mutual fund, I'd ask, What's my rate of return over five years? But this was entirely different. The rate of return in this instance was a matter of life and death."

It was a crisis situation and he didn't have much time to think. Over lunch, at a mall across the street from one of the doctor's offices, Lance made his decision. He chose brain surgery. Eventually, he was completely cured and his lungs were not affected. The choice he made saved not only his life, but also his cycling career. A few short years later, he went on to win the Tour de France. Even though many people said it was a fluke, he proved them wrong by winning again year after year. Lance Armstrong has now won the Tour de France a staggering *seven times in a row*. He is the first man in history to win the Tour de France seven times and the first to do it seven times in a row! This is an accomplishment that may not be duplicated for another two hundred years. This is an incredible feat for anyone, but even more incredible considering that he was once lying in a hospital room dying of cancer. The day after he won his fifth Tour de France, he was in Portugal speaking at the National Cancer Institute's International Cancer Panel.

The decision behind the decision here is critical. It is the decision of where to go for advice. This decision is as important as the decision itself. When you ask others for advice, remember that no one evaluating the situation is completely unbiased. Sometimes the advice we get from various important people in our lives is inconsistent.

For example, one of your religious leaders might tell you not to get a divorce because it is a sin. On the other hand, your psychiatrist might tell you it is the best thing for your mental and emotional well-being. Is one right and the other wrong? Not necessarily. Each one is an expert in his or her own field. You just have to keep in mind that each person's education, training, and life's experiences have influenced their thinking and how they view your situation.

Even the most objective scientists, doctors, engineers and Ph.D.'s are not immune from the Fourth Law of Critical

Focus™: *We tend to see what we're expecting to see.* Archeologist Albert Goodyear of the University of South Carolina explains, "Scientists tend to see what they expect to see, and when they see something they don't expect, they are sometimes slow to change their point of view."

Sometimes what the experts tell us is just plain wrong. Today they tell us that oat bran reduces cholesterol. Tomorrow they tell us "but not much." Today they tell us that an aspirin a day reduces the risk of heart attacks and strokes. Tomorrow they tell us "not really." Even the world-famous physicist and Pulitzer Prize winner Stephen Hawking told us a few years ago that nothing could escape the power of the gravity within a "black hole." If something went into it, it would never come out. Today he tells us, "never mind."

When you are impressed with the credentials and advice of an important person in your life, don't forget to consider the source from which they speak. We tend to view our present experiences in light of the things we have experienced in the past. These past experiences shade our view of life as though we were wearing uniquely colored glasses. These glasses cause us to view all present and future experiences, *even those of others*, in light of what we have experienced. A person speaks out of instincts born of his or her own past experience, education, and training.

Don't forget that you have to do your own research and come to your own conclusions. Don't ever take anyone's advice solely because of who they are or because you are afraid that they will be offended if you don't. It is *your* life. You, not they, will have to live with the consequences of your own decision.

Is it wise to consult *only* those who share your view of the world to the exclusion of all others? In his book *All Rivers Run to the Sea*, Nobel Peace Laureate Elie Wiesel describes his childhood home, nestled in the little town of Sighet, Hungary. One day in 1938, a series of decrees was issued in Sighet. By order of military command, all stores and offices belonging to Jews were closed. No Jew was allowed to go out, except in the late afternoon to buy food. Jews no longer had the right to sell anything. Anyone who opposed these decrees would be shot. The German army began raiding Jewish homes, taking jewelry, silver, foreign currency, and precious stones — anything of value.

Then came the announcement that a ghetto was to be created for the Jews in Sighet. The Wiesel family had a housekeeper named Maria, who was a Christian. Maria had worked for the family for many years and was like part of the family. While the Wiesel family was in the ghetto, Maria somehow managed to make it through the barricades and barbed wire to bring them cheese, eggs, fruit, and vegetables. Maria had a cabin in a remote location in the mountains. When the first transports began to take the Jews away to an "unknown place," Maria begged the Wiesel family to escape from the ghetto and go with her to live in the cabin, where they would not be found.

One night, the Wiesel family gathered at the kitchen table and held a family meeting. Should they follow Maria or stay? This critical decision would shape the rest of their lives. At that time, the Wiesel family and most Jews in Europe were not aware of the horrors that awaited them. Maria's offer to help the Wiesel family escape went against the advice of the city's intellectuals, dignitaries, and clergy, whose views were that the Jewish community should stay together as much as possible. The irony is that in the final analysis the Nazis ripped the Jewish community apart anyway.

After much pleading and begging by Maria, the Wiesel family declined her invitation on the basis that "a Jew must never be separated from his community." Elie's father, as head of the household, explained to Maria: "What happens to everyone else will happen to us as well." When Mrs. Wiesel suggested that at least the children should go with Maria, the children protested. "We're young and strong. The trip won't be as dangerous for us. If anyone should go with Maria, it's you," they told their mother. That was the last evening the Wiesels spent together as a family. The next day they were transported to concentration camps, where most of the members of Elie Wiesel's family suffered unspeakable horrors and death.

This moving story illustrates how the conventional wisdom of those who share our belief system does not always yield the best answer. Sometimes the best advice comes from an unlikely source — in this case, from a Christian housekeeper in the middle of a Jewish community. She was the only one capable of thinking "outside the box" because she was the only one who was already outside the box, both literally and figuratively.

"Those whose interests are threatened by extreme danger should think only of the wisest course of action, not of convention."

— ROMAN EMPRESS THEODORA

In a crisis situation, the most dangerous thing you can do is to go *only* to those people who think like you do for advice. Why? Because if they share your same belief system, they most likely also share your same blind spots. If there are any errors in your thinking, those who think like you do are the *least* qualified to point it out. They are in the same box you are in. When you are trying to make a critical decision, go to someone who is *already* outside the box.

In many cases, the decision of who to go to for advice is the most important factor that will determine your final decision. Therefore, when contemplating any piece of advice, consider the source. Are people recommending a certain course of action because they are programmed to think the way they do? Have they been in your shoes? Have they truly thought out your situation in terms of what is best *for you*?

Does the person who is giving you advice understand all the factors that are important to you? Do they know how the effects of following their advice will trickle down to other parts of your life? Have they given a fair evaluation of other options available to you? Have they considered how you may have changed over the years? Do they have a good grasp of the up and downsides of each of your alternatives? Do they understand the severity of the situation you find yourself in? Do they understand the consequences of each choice? Do they have all the facts that you have?

Close your eyes. Take a moment to be still and quiet. Imagine that you have chosen one of your options. What kind of feelings do you experience when you imagine yourself doing what you are about to do? Next, visualize every aspect of a typical day after you have made your choice, from the time you wake up to the time you go to bed. Envision the setting in detail. What do you see? What do you hear? What do you smell? Do you like your environment? What is the first thing you will do that day? What is the second, the third, and so on? Envision the people around you. What kind of people are they? Are they loud and brash? Are they quiet and intellectual? Are they responsible and competent? Are they trustworthy? Do they share common interests with you? Do they respect and admire you? Do you respect and admire them? Now take all of this information and examine your heart. How do you feel now about the decision you are about to make? Weigh this against the advice you've received from friends, family, and mentors. But always trust your instincts. Never betray your heart.

Above all, do what is right for you. Don't rely on an expert just because he or she has all the right documents hanging on the office wall. There are other experts out there with equally impressive credentials if you will just seek them out. Heroes become heroes because they can see through the smoke enough to make their own educated decisions after objectively weighing all of the options.

> THE DECISION BEHIND THE DECISION:
> Heroes CHOOSE their experts cautiously,
> knowing that no one comes to the table
> truly unbiased.

HEROES KNOW THEY CAN'T SEE THE WHOLE PARADE

"There is nothing good nor bad,
but thinking makes it so."
— WILLIAM SHAKESPEARE

Sometimes we create a crisis in our mind when there is no external, objective evidence of crisis. There is a children's story about a chicken called Henny Penny that can teach us a great deal about self-created crisis. When an acorn fell on Henny Penny's head she panicked because she thought to herself, "The sky is falling." She told all her friends and neighbors the sky was falling and described the evidence she had to prove it. An acorn had fallen on her head. All of her friends accepted her story as true and were convinced that the sky really was falling. One by one, they were overcome by emotion and they panicked. In their panic, they went to the fox for help. The fox asked them to trust him, which, of course, they did. Ultimately, the fox ate them all.

Indeed, for Henny Penny and her friends, the sky *had* fallen. They had created a self-fulfilling prophecy. They had acted as though what they believed was real and, by their very actions, they brought it to pass. Their false perception of reality produced an irrational decision, which *itself* proved to be their undoing.

Like Henny Penny, we sometimes create our own crisis because we are *expecting* one. But, as the story indicates, nothing has any significance of its own. Everything has only the significance that *we give it*. Some things that happen in our lives are like a double-edged sword. It is possible for them to work for us or against us, depending on how we interpret them and react to them. Almost everything is a matter of interpretation.

> *"Men are not disturbed by things that happen,*
> *but by their opinion of things that happen."*
> — Epictetus

Sometimes in our careers or relationships, we are tempted to make decisions too soon in situations that don't require immediate action. We don't like the situation we are in. We are impatient. We can't stand it any longer. We must make a decision — NOW! Something strange happens at work and we interpret it in the worst possible light. We assume we are about to be fired or transferred or demoted. Then we feel compelled to quickly consider all of our other options and make a decision as soon as possible.

If you constantly see evil motives where there are none, people will come to know you as an accuser and a cynical, overly suspicious person. Think about it. Would you want to hang around this kind of person for very long? If you quit your job or end a relationship every time you have a problem, you may ultimately be unemployed and have very few friends. Sometimes the best thing we can do is remain calm and make a decision to "wait and see."

*"Trying to understand is like straining
to see through muddy water. Be still,
and allow the mud to settle. Remain
still, until it is the time to act."*

— LAO TZU

Writer Joel Achenbach of the *Washington Post* tells of a true story that happened on the morning of September 11, 2001. A civilian aircraft had just crashed into the Pentagon. Smoke was pouring out of the building and could be seen for miles. Washington, D.C. was in a state of emergency. Rumors were flying all around that the city was under attack. But less than two miles away, there was a man sitting on a park bench, quietly reading the newspaper. Achenbach saw him sitting there and asked him if he knew what was going on. The man said yes, but that he had no interest in joining any evacuation or even listening to the latest news bulletin. He figured he was in no danger and everything would return to normal soon.

Why didn't the man flee? Why didn't he panic? Psychologists tell us that people process risk and danger in two different ways: one way is intuitive/emotional and the other is logical/analytical. The intuitive process is based on images from our past experience that have been seared into our subconscious. In some cases, the objective facts show no danger, but our gut tells us that something doesn't "feel right." I have heard lieutenants who fought in Vietnam relay stories from personal experience about how they made decisions during the heat of battle based on gut instinct alone that ended up saving the lives of their men. When faced with extreme danger, sometimes our intuition takes over for the better. But this can backfire. In everyday life, sometimes our feelings can cause us to make illogical choices. Our feelings sometimes muddle our analysis and our ability to see things as they really are.

Psychologist Paul Slovic of the University of Oregon says, "You need your feelings to put a cross-check on your analysis, and you need analysis to keep your feelings in check." The point is, we shouldn't let our feelings take over, but we shouldn't ignore them either.

Sometimes we need to take a break and take a big step backwards to see the big picture. We don't always know immediately whether something will turn out to be good or bad for us. I once heard a preacher (and later Anthony Robbins) tell a story about a man whose horse ran away. His neighbors said, "Oh, that's bad." Then the horse returned with two other horses. The neighbors said, "That's good." Then the man's son fell off one of the new horses and broke his leg. The neighbors said, "That's bad." A war erupted and the army took away all of the healthy young men, but the man's son was spared because of his broken leg. The neighbors said, "That's good."

Here's a real-life example. In the 1950s in Madrid, a young man named Julio achieved his greatest dream of becoming a goalkeeper for a professional soccer team called Real Madrid. But his dreams were shattered when a near-fatal car accident left him partially paralyzed and unable to walk for almost two years. During his hospital stay, he would listen to the radio and write poems, most of which were sad and questioned whether life had any meaning.

A friend of his father gave him an old guitar as therapy to exercise his fingers and pass the time. He began to dress up his poems with music as he strummed away on the old guitar. A passion for music began to well up within him and eventually took over his life. In 1968, Julio surprised everyone, including himself, by winning the most prestigious song festival in Spain with his own composition called *La Vida Sigue Igual.*

From that point on, Julio continued to compose music, and eventually he became an international superstar. By 1971, he had sold his first million records. By 1973, he broke the record for the number of awards won by any music star in Spain and all of Latin America. His concerts consistently broke box office records. In 1983, the *Guinness Book of World Records* gave him the Diamond Record Award for selling more records in more languages than any other musical artist in history. It was the first and only such award ever given. His first English release in 1984 went multi-platinum and formed an all-important bridge between European and American music. In 1985, a star with his name was unveiled on the Hollywood Walk of Fame.

His *full name* is Julio Iglesias. He has achieved over 2,600 platinum and gold record certifications and has sold over two hundred million records around the world. His son, Enrique Iglesias, now follows in his footsteps.

> *"Weeping may endure for a night,*
> *but joy comes in the morning."*
> — PSALM 30:5

What is happening to you may be bad right now but may turn out to be good later. Sometimes the importance of an event isn't revealed until enough time has passed and we see the full picture. It is said that time heals all wounds. Perhaps it is because in time we come to understand events that we did not understand when they first occurred. The passage of time allows for all of the pieces to fit together. Heroes know that they may not be able to see all the pieces just yet.

Sometimes I imagine that we, as people, are standing like children watching a parade through the knotholes of a tall wooden privacy fence. We cannot see the beginning or the end of the parade. We can only see the events as they pass right before us through the knothole. Because of our limited perspective, we cannot see the whole picture. We can only live one day at a time. How can we know whether something is a disaster or a miracle until we've seen the whole parade, the beginning and the end? Heroes know they can't see the whole parade.

Sometimes the best decision is to wait and see. Use your family and friends as a reality check. Do your closest friends and family share your perception that something terrible will happen if you don't act quickly? Remember, they act as mirrors or sounding boards in our lives, and they can reflect back to us whether we are behaving rationally. However, remember to choose your sounding boards wisely. Go only to people you trust, people who have your best interest at heart. Don't go to the "fox" for advice. Always consider the source.

When we have feelings of desperation, we, like Henny Penny, may find ourselves considering options we would not normally consider because we are in a panic. Take a moment to calm down. Go on a vacation. Take a weekend off. Do something fun to distract yourself from the decision for a while.

One of my favorite things to do when I'm in the middle of making a stressful decision is to take a long drive in the country. I go to a quaint small town near Austin, Texas, called Wimberley, which is on the beautiful, lazy Cypress Creek. Giant cypress trees shoot up from the banks of the crystal-blue stream below, and children jump into the waters from low-lying branches, laughing at the world as they go. Things move slowly in small towns. People are friendly. They are not in a hurry. The atmosphere is very relaxed. Stress just seems to float off my shoulders. Sometimes I go camping or to the mountains to ponder the universe and the impact of a decision I am about to make.

I also run regularly to clear my mind and to relieve stress. I have friends who cycle thirty to forty miles at a time and others who run five to ten miles regularly. They tell me the exercise gives them time away from the stress of making difficult decisions. Sometimes when they are running, ideas come to them that help them resolve difficult issues. Sometimes our brain becomes paralyzed from the stress of worrying about a problem too much, and we need to give ourselves a mental break.

Garrison Keillor, author of the book *Lake Wobegon Days* and creator and host of the very popular radio show, "A Prairie Home Companion," made a surprising decision to retire the show at the height of its success. Later, Keillor stated: "I did the wrong thing, looking back. It certainly worked out well, but now I'm in the position where I can give advice to people, and one piece of advice is, 'Don't make decisions when you're tired. Make them at the end of a three-week vacation.' "

The wisdom of this statement had been expressed centuries before by one of the greatest thinkers in history:

> "Every now and then go away, have a little relaxation, for when you come back to your work your judgment will be surer; since to remain constantly at work will cause you to lose power of judgment ... go some distance away because the work appears smaller and more of it can be taken in at a glance, and a lack of harmony or proportion is more readily seen."
>
> — LEONARDO DA VINCI

After several years of taking a break, Keillor renewed the radio show. It is now hugely successful again, and he has been offered parts in commercials, movies, and plays.

Remember also that if you make a decision too soon, you may end up settling for something less than best just to get yourself out of the situation you find yourself in. Ultimately this can lead to frustration because you may be going against your better judgment. You may find yourself wanting to bail out again very soon. It is easy to fall prey to the "grass is greener on the other side" syndrome instead of being patient and making the best of the situation.

Lance Armstrong said, "It's too tempting, in the throes of it, to quit on any problem that seems hard or inconvenient, to call it a waste of precious time and move on to something more immediate. Some things require patience."

At some point, you may need to make a decision to hang in there and learn all you can from your current situation, no matter how bad it may seem. This builds character and discipline and teaches you responsibility. In the meantime, something better may come along when you have learned what you are supposed to have learned from your current situation. Remember, *you can learn something good from every situation in life, no matter how difficult.* But you have to look for it. It may be lying just beneath the rubble. Be patient.

In addition, sometimes because of how much we have grown, we are able to face future problems with greater ease. Remember, diamonds are just rocks that are formed under intense heat and pressure deep within the earth. Without the heat and intense pressure, they would just be rocks. If you continue to run from the pressure, you may never become the person you are supposed to become. Heroes become heroes by holding their ground until the battle is over. Sometimes the last person standing wins. Sometimes the best decision is to stand still. Sometimes it is best to "wait and see."

THE DECISION BEHIND THE DECISION:
Heroes CHOOSE to take a step back because
they know they can't see the whole parade
from where they stand.

HEROES CAN SEE STARS BEYOND COCONUTS

"There is no freedom until we acquire the power
to choose how we respond to outside forces."
— DR. GERALD MANN

One of the most powerful principles you can take from this book is that you do have a choice. Many people feel trapped in their current situation. They feel that there is no way out and they are doomed to a life of misery and frustration. This is a desperate feeling. It might be a bad employment situation. It might be a bad personal relationship. If you learn anything from this book, learn that you don't have to stay where you are. You weren't destined to be miserable. You should abandon any set of beliefs that compels you to stay on a course that is destroying your spirit, limiting who you are, or not allowing you to fulfill your best and highest purpose in life.

You are not condemned to live the rest of your life based on choices you made in the past. Life is a process of growing and learning. Our spirit and character never stops developing. A choice that was right for us yesterday may not be right for us today. You don't have to keep wearing last year's clothes if they no longer fit. You don't have to keep wearing styles that you looked good in five years ago. Just because they looked good on you then doesn't mean they look good on you now. Take a long look in the mirror. Things may have changed. *You* may have changed.

The people you used to be close to may have grown in different directions from you. You may have hobbies or interests today that you didn't have a few years ago. These new interests and hobbies may have led you to an entirely new group of friends and places you had never been before. This is okay. This is a part of the normal evolutionary process of growing. Life is fluid, not stagnant. If you ever stop growing, it'll be because you're dead. It's a very liberating feeling when you realize that you have choices. Now that you know the truth, it's up to you. Will you choose to stay where you are or will you start moving in the direction you want to take?

Our mind is the steering wheel of our lives. No matter what the subject is, if you *focus* on it long enough, your entire life will eventually turn in that direction. Just try driving a car in a forward direction while you are looking at a 90-degree angle to your left for sixty seconds. If you have ever stared off to the left for more than a few seconds, you know what happens. Your car will start to drift to the left, whether you like it or not. It is impossible to keep the car going straight when you are looking off in another direction.

You get the point. Control what you think about and you can control the direction your life takes. Control what you read, what you watch, and who you associate with, and you can control how you think and feel. You can begin reshaping your life today simply by reading about, studying, and pouring your energies in the direction you want your life to go. Your mind is a multimillion-dollar software program that controls every aspect of your life. You have the freedom and the power to program that software to do whatever you choose. But first you must make a decision. Start *deliberately focusing* your mind on the direction in which you want your life to go, and you will see things you never saw before.

Remember — if you can imagine it, you can achieve it. If our mind is like the computer that controls every function of our life, then it follows that it can be programmed to achieve whatever vision we have provided it. For example, there was a point in time when the thought of flying was more of a joke than even a fantasy. Then it became a fantasy. Then it became someone's dream. Next it became someone's goal. Then it became someone's obsession. Finally, through hard work, creativity, persistence, and trial and error, it became a reality. Now flying is a commonplace event. Now you can earn frequent flyer miles as a reward for flying often! I flew to Africa a few years ago. It took approximately twenty-two hours and I thought that was a long time. Imagine that! It took less than twenty-four hours to travel across the world in a hunk of steel suspended in air! What would Christopher Columbus think? How can this be? Was it luck? Was it destined to be? No. This was just the practical outcome of a universal truth: If you can imagine it, you can achieve it.

> *"Whatever you can do, or dream you can, begin it.*
> *Boldness has genius, power, and magic in it."*
> — W.H. MURRAY

Consider the telephone. Does it ever fascinate you how you can hear the voices of those you love as though they were standing in the same room, even though they may be thousands of miles away? The next time you talk to someone you love on the phone, listen to the sound of their breathing or sighing or yawning. Think of the times you have laughed or cried with someone on the phone. You can feel what they are feeling and empathize with what they are experiencing as though you were right there with them. Two hundred years ago, who would have imagined that we would be able to convey our thoughts and feelings to another person electronically over a pair of wires? The most common use of wires two hundred years ago was tying fences together. Before the telephone was invented, the *Boston Post* ran an article that said, "Well-informed people know that it is impossible to transmit voice over a pair of wires." Now you can communicate laughter, sorrow, fear, anger, sadness, and joy over a thin pair of wires. You can even hear people sigh and yawn. What's even more amazing is that now we can even do it without wires!

> *"The greater danger for most of us is not that our aim is too high and we miss it, but that it is too low and we reach it."*
>
> — MICHELANGELO

Think of your favorite TV show for a minute. Do you really understand how they can transmit moving visual images of real people doing real things through thin air all the way around the globe? I have often wondered, where are those images when they are traveling through the air? How do satellites really work? Every time you pick up the phone, turn on your air conditioner, get in your car, check your e-mail, watch TV, or fly in an airplane, you are living someone else's dream. Just a short one hundred years ago, we didn't have any of this technology. Who knows what we will be experiencing in the future that we cannot even imagine today? We aren't limited to what we have experienced in the past or what we are experiencing today. We are limited only by our minds.

The same is true in your life. You are not limited by the experiences of your past. You do not have to stay where you are, but you do have to make a choice to accept this principle: If you can imagine it, you can achieve it. Do you really believe this? What is the world waiting for you to imagine? What is the world waiting for you to achieve? If you don't do it, it may never get done. You owe it not only to yourself, but to the world. This may be your life's calling.

> *"If you limit your choices only to what seems possible or reasonable, you disconnect yourself from what you truly want, and all that is left is a compromise."*
>
> — ROBERT FRITZ

Albert Einstein once said, "Imagination is more important than knowledge." When I first read this quote, I was puzzled. Albert Einstein was not an artist, a musician, or an author. He did not make his living by being creative or imaginative. He was a scientist who required hard evidence to support his theories. Yet he considered his ability to imagine things he *could not see* to be more important than the things he *could see*. Perhaps Einstein understood that human knowledge is limited to what can enter the brain through the five senses — tangible things we can see, hear, smell, taste, touch, weigh, and measure. But imagination is unlimited because it is not restricted to what we can see, hear, touch, or even to what we can understand. Our imagination has no boundaries. It is infinite. Coming from Einstein, this is a very profound statement. Heroes *see* things that others do not see.

> *"Imagination is the real and eternal world of which this vegetable universe is but a faint shadow . . . the eternal body of man is the imagination: that is God himself, the Divine body . . ."*
>
> — WILLIAM BLAKE

Einstein and all of the great inventors, including Leonardo Da Vinci, Thomas Edison, Alexander Graham Bell, and Benjamin Franklin, saw what no one else saw because they chose to exercise the power of their imagination. They understood that our imagination is usually four or five steps ahead of the reach of our knowledge and experience. But through hard work, determination, and creative experimenting, our reality is usually able to find a way to catch up to our imagination.

> *"The most beautiful thing we can experience is the mysterious. It is the source of all true art and science."*
>
> — ALBERT EINSTEIN

Keep chasing your dreams. You will eventually catch them. Henry David Thoreau said, "If you have built castles in the air, your work need not be lost; that is where they should be. Now put the foundations under them."

Man's walk on the moon started as "castles in the air" until man built the foundation under them. Now trips to the moon and beyond are routine. One of my favorite quotes comes from the movie *Toy Story*, in which the action figure Buzz Lightyear exclaims, "To infinity and beyond!" I have a Buzz Lightyear action figure in my office to remind me of

this motto. Let this become your life's motto and there may
be no end to what you can accomplish.

On a recent trip to the beautiful island of Maui, I went
for a long walk along the beach just in time to see the last
light of sunset. The sun had just slipped under the horizon.
The horizon was still glowing a red-orange hue beneath a
deep blue sky. A crescent moon, thin as a hair, winked at me
from the southwest. I sat down to watch the orange glow on
the horizon melt into the night. After dark, on the way back
I found a hammock strung between two coconut trees and
lay down in it. The coconut trees must have been at least
sixty feet tall.

I began to imagine how ancient man, with few or no
tools, must have looked up one day and prayed for a way
to get to the tops of the coconut trees in order to get to the
coconuts. Coconut trees get thinner as they get taller and
they have no branches except at the very top. To primitive
man, it must have seemed an impossible feat to get to the
top. As I stared at the coconuts, the stars in the night sky
beyond the coconuts were quietly smiling at me. I hadn't
noticed them at first because I was too busy thinking
about the coconuts. When I finally started *focusing* on the
stars, they seemed to be shouting, "Hey! We're up here!"
Then I imagined how, just a few short years ago, modern
man might have finally started praying for a way to reach
the stars!

I realized in my own life, too often I pray for a way to
reach the tops of the coconut trees when I should be praying
to reach the stars. It's a matter of perspective. When we look
up, we can either *focus* on the coconuts or look beyond the
coconuts to the stars. Before we can seriously consider the

stars, we have to expand the parameters of our mind. Behavioral scientists teach us that we tend to see only what we are *focusing* on and not what is really there. Similarly, history teaches that man usually reaches the level of his expectations and no more.

As I contemplated this phenomenon, it occurred to me that when we pray, we should remember who it is we are asking. The name by which we call Him is irrelevant. The point is, are we praying to the God of the universe or the God of the coconuts? When we remember who it is we are asking, the realm of realistic possibilities is expanded by a quantum leap. God is not limited by anything. But what we can expect from God is limited by what we *focus* on. Therefore, we should make a conscious *decision* to focus on the stars. The stars are a reminder of who it is we are asking and how big He is, and therefore, how big the realm of possibilities is. Let the earth dwellers have the coconuts.

> *"There are two ways to live; one is as though nothing is a miracle. The other is as if everything is."*
>
> — ALBERT EINSTEIN

No matter what you have achieved in the past, you've only just begun. No matter how great your victories have been in the past, they serve only as evidence of what you *could* accomplish in the future. Don't ever be satisfied with last year's victories. Last year's victories don't pay today's bills. Last year's victories don't fulfill tomorrow's dreams. Keep on dreaming. Keep on reaching for the stars. Eventually, you'll catch them.

But it all starts with a decision. Like every hero in this book, you have the power to *choose* what you will focus on. What you *focus* on determines what you believe. What you *believe* determines what you expect. What you *expect* determines what you *see*. What you *see* determines what options are available to you. You have the power to *choose* what to focus on, no matter what is going on in the world around you.

Put this book down now, and do something. Make something happen. Do something out of the ordinary. Put down the map you have been following and look at the trail you are on. Read the soil, the crushed grass, the twigs, and the fallen leaves. Reach down to feel the soil and the soft grass. Sit down for a while. Take time to look around. Study each individual branch in the trees above you. Then lie down on your back and look up. Look way up ... beyond the trees ... and focus on the stars ...

Perhaps they're trying to tell you something.

THE DECISION BEHIND THE DECISION:
Heroes CHOOSE to focus on stars
rather than coconuts.

HEAR DAN SPEAK!
Go to www.dancastro.com for sample audio!

Dear Meeting Planner: *If you are looking for a keynote speaker for your next event, please keep Dan Castro in mind.*

Dan is available for all speaking events from 30 minute keynotes to full weekend interactive workshops, facilitation and training.

Whether you hire Dan for half an hour or a full weekend, your audience will come away with valuable tools for resolving conflict, finding creative solutions to problems, awakening the senses to see new insights, achieving goals and motivating their staff.

If you have any questions, please call me at 1-800-531-3789.

Sincerely,

HEATHER MAUL, *Executive Assistant to Dan Castro*

SPEAKING/TRAINING TOPICS INCLUDE:

1) THE SEVEN LAWS OF CRITICAL FOCUS™

2) THE DECISION BEHIND THE DECISION™

3) THE HERO'S PATH™

4) CRITICAL CHOICES THAT CHANGE LIVES™

5) HOW LEADERS BECOME LEGENDS™

6) HOW TO PURSUE YOUR PASSION AND STILL PAY THE RENT

7) SEVEN WAYS TO TURN PAST FAILURES INTO SPRINGBOARDS FOR SUCCESS

8) WHAT TO DO AFTER THE "BIG DEAL" FALLS THROUGH

9) WHY OUR EXPECTATIONS DETERMINE WHAT WE SEE OR DON'T SEE

10) IT'S NOT WHAT YOU SEE, IT'S HOW YOU SEE IT

11) WHY IMAGINATION IS MORE IMPORTANT THAN KNOWLEDGE

12) WHY THE OBSTACLE STANDING IN YOUR WAY IS NOT THE BIGGEST OBSTACLE

13) THE PATTERNS THAT HEROES HAVE FOLLOWED FOR THOUSANDS OF YEARS TO OVERCOME EXTREME OBSTACLES

14) HOW HEROES THROUGHOUT HISTORY IDENTIFIED THEIR PASSION

15) WHAT TO DO AFTER YOU'VE BEEN BETRAYED

16) WHAT LEGENDARY LEADERS SEE THAT THE REST OF US DON'T

17) HOW TO SEE BEYOND THE LIMITS OF YOUR OWN EXPECTATIONS

18) WHY YOU CAN'T SEE THE WHOLE PARADE FROM WHERE YOU STAND

We look forward to hearing from you!

About the Author

Daniel R. Castro is a business litigation attorney and partner in the law firm of Castro & Baker, LLP, in Austin, Texas. Dan is an honors graduate of the University of Texas School of Law. He has spent the last twenty-five years mentoring teenagers and law students. Professionally, Dan has represented Fortune 500 corporations in multimillion-dollar litigation, individual corporate executives in employment disputes, and small to mid-size corporations in hotly contested commercial and real estate disputes.

Aside from practicing law, Dan is also a professional keynote speaker, executive retreat leader, and executive trainer. Dan is also a business strategist/business consultant, helping clients to find the best strategy for starting businesses, developing business plans, building businesses, and solving problems.

Dan has an insatiable love of history and has always gravitated toward the stories of people who seemed to prosper in the midst of crisis and adversity when everyone else around them failed. He was curious about what set these people apart and made them heroes. After he started practicing law, Dan started conducting the research that went into *Critical Choices That Change Lives*. His natural curiosity led him on a ten-year adventure of reading volumes of biographies, academic articles, psychological treatises, magazines, newspapers, and observing people. What he discovered was that heroes are people who can literally see and hear things around them that other people cannot. But what gives them the ability to see and hear things that others cannot?

Dan collected all of these stories, pulled out the patterns and principles, and laid them out for all to see. The result is *Critical Choices That Change Lives*.

ORDER FORM

Use this convenient form to order additional
copies of *Critical Choices That Change Lives*

BY PHONE: (800)531-3789

ORDER ONLINE:
www.dancastro.com

FAX this form to (512)732-0115

E-MAIL request for books to:
hmauel@gmail.com

Please send me_____ copies @ $14.95 each $_____
(call for bulk order discounts)

Postage and handling (add $3.95 for the $_____
first book and $2 for each additional book)

Texas residents add 8.25% tax $_____

Total $_____

❑ Enclosed is my check (payable to Beartooth Press)

Please charge my credit card #_____

❑ Visa   ❑ MasterCard   ❑ American Express   exp. date_____

please print

Name_____

Address_____

_____

City_____ State_____ Zip_____

Phone (   )_____

E-mail_____